DAVID COPPERFIELD

Interweaving Truth and Fiction

TWAYNE'S MASTERWORK STUDIES

Robert Lecker, General Editor

DAVID COPPERFIELD

Interweaving Truth and Fiction

GRAHAM STOREY

Twayne Publishers • Boston
A DIVISION OF G. K. HALL & CO.

David Copperfield: Interweaving Truth and Fiction
Graham Storey

Twayne's Masterwork Studies No. 68
Copyright 1991 by G. K. Hall & Co.
All rights reserved.
Published by Twayne Publishers
A division of G. K. Hall & Co.
70 Lincoln Street
Boston, Massachusetts 02111

Copyediting supervised by Barbara Sutton.
Book production by Gabrielle B. McDonald.
Typeset in Sabon with Electra display type
by Compset, Inc. of Beverly, Massachusetts.

10 9 8 7 6 5 4 3 2 1 (hc)
10 9 8 7 6 5 4 3 2 1 (pb)

Library of Congress Cataloging-in-Publication Data

Storey, Graham, 1920–
    David Copperfield : interweaving truth and fiction / Graham
Storey.
        p.   cm.—(Twayne's masterwork studies ; no. 68)
    Includes bibliographical references and index.
    ISBN 0-8057-9415-8 (hc.)—ISBN 0-8057-8142-0 (pbk)
    1. Dickens, Charles, 1812–1870. David Copperfield. I. Title.
II. Series.
PR4558.S76   1991
823'.8—dc20   90-22091
                                                                    CIP

Contents

Historical and Literary Context

A Reading

Note on the References and Acknowledgments

All page references are to the New Oxford Illustrated Dickens edition (Oxford, 1948; latest reprint, 1987), with the original illustrations by "Phiz" (H. K. Browne), based on the Charles Dickens Edition of 1867; this edition, revised by Dickens, was the first to be given descriptive headlines. First published in monthly serial parts from May 1849 to November 1850, *David Copperfield* was issued in book form, in one volume, in November 1850. The most scholarly edition, the Clarendon Dickens (1981), was edited by Nina Burgis; it gives Dickens's 17 trial titles, his number plans (often drawn on in this study), and all the passages, some of them lengthy and important, deleted by Dickens in proof—all taken from manuscripts in the Forster Collection in the Victoria and Albert Museum, London.

Charles Dickens in December 1852.
From a photograph by John E. Mayall.
Reproduced by permission of the Dickens House Museum, London.

Chronology: Charles Dickens's Life and Works

1812	Charles John Huffam Dickens is born 7 February at 13 Mile End Terrace, Portsea, Hampshire, the second child of John Dickens (?1785–1851), an improvident clerk in the Navy Pay Office, and Elizabeth (1789–1863), daughter of Charles Barrow, formerly also in the Navy Pay Office, until he embezzled over £5,000 of Navy funds.
1820	Enrolled in the Rev. William Giles's School, Chatham, Kent.
1824	Works for about 12 months, probably February 1824–February 1825, in Jonathan Warren's blacking-warehouse, Hungerford Stairs, Strand, during his father's imprisonment for debt in the Marshalsea. Lives in lodgings, first in Little College Street, Camden Town, then in Lant Street, Southwark, near the Marshalsea.
ca. 1825–1826	Enrolled at Wellington House Academy, Hampstead Road (the Salem House of *David Copperfield*).
1827	Works as solicitor's clerk. Learns Gurney's system of shorthand, "that savage stenographic mystery" (*David Copperfield*, Chapter 43).
1828–1832	Works as reporter in Doctors' Commons.
1830–1833	Has unsuccessful and anguished love affair with Maria Beadnell, daughter of a prosperous banker.
1832	Works as parliamentary reporter on the *True Sun* and on his uncle J. H. Barrow's *The Mirror of Parliament*.
1833	Anonymously, publishes his first sketch, "A Dinner at Poplar Walk," in *Monthly Magazine* 1 December.
1834	Works as staff reporter on *Morning Chronicle*. Publishes more sketches.
1835	Reports election nominations and speeches.

DAVID COPPERFIELD

1836	Publishes *Sketches by Boz,* illustrated by George Cruikshank and H. K. Browne ("Phiz") 8 February. "Boz" taken from his youngest brother Augustus's mispronunciation of his nickname, Moses).
1836–1837	Publishes, in 20 monthly installments, *The Pickwick Papers,* illustrated by Robert Seymour, who commits suicide after seven plates; R. W. Buss illustrates no. 3, and "Phiz" the remainder.
	Marries Catherine Hogarth, daughter of George Hogarth, distinguished music critic and former friend of Sir Walter Scott, 2 April. Sets up house in 15 Furnival's Inn, Holborn.
	His farce, *The Strange Gentleman,* and operetta *The Village Coquettes* (music by John Hullah), produced 29 September and 6 December at St. James's Theater, London.
	Meets John Forster, who becomes his closest friend and biographer, in December.
1837	Victoria, aged 18, succeeds to the throne of England 20 June.
1837–1839	Edits *Bentley's Miscellany. Oliver Twist,* illustrated by Cruikshank, published in *Bentley's Miscellany.*
1837	Birth of Charles Culliford Boz Dickens, his first child, 6 January. Moves to 48 Doughty Street (now the Dickens House Museum) in April. Mary Hogarth, Catherine's next younger sister, aged 17, dies 7 May, with shocking suddenness, in his arms, in Doughty Street. Carlyle's *The French Revolution* published.
1838–1839	*Nicholas Nickleby,* illustrated by "Phiz," published.
1839	Moves to 1 Devonshire Terrace, York Gate, Regent's Park, in December. First Chartist riots.
1840	Queen Victoria marries Prince Albert of Saxe-Coburg-Gotha.
1840–1841	*Master Humphrey's Clock,* containing *The Old Curiosity Shop* and *Barnaby Rudge,* illustrated by George Cattermole and "Phiz," published.
1841	*Punch* founded; edited by Dickens's friend, Mark Lemon.
1842	First visit to America, with Catherine, January to June, ending with a month in Canada.
1842	*American Notes,* which, together with the American chapters of *Martin Chuzzlewit,* causes much ill feeling against him by many Americans, including some former friends, published October.
1842–1843	*Martin Chuzzlewit,* illustrated by "Phiz," published.

Chronology

1843	His first Christmas book, *A Christmas Carol*, illustrated by John Leech, published December.
1844	*The Chimes*, illustrated by Daniel Maclise, John Leech, Richard Doyle, and Clarkson Stanfield, published December. Directs and acts in amateur production of Jonson's *Every Man in His Humour*.
1844–1845	Travels in Italy with Catherine, the children, and his sister-in-law, Georgina Hogarth. This tour provides most of the material used later for *Pictures from Italy* (1846), illustrated by Samuel Palmer.
1845	*The Cricket on the Hearth*, illustrated by Maclise, Leech, Doyle, and Stanfield, published December.
1846	Launches the *Daily News*; John Forster takes over as editor after two and a half weeks. Travels in Switzerland and Paris with Catherine, the children, and Georgina Hogarth from May to December.
	Writes *The Life of Our Lord*, a version of the Gospels, for his children (not intended for publication, it is finally published in 1934). The *Battle of Life*, illustrated by Maclise, Leech, Doyle, and Stanfield, published December.
1846–1847	*Dombey and Son*, illustrated by "Phiz," published.
1847	Charlotte Brontë's *Jane Eyre* published. Angela Burdett-Coutts's Home for Homeless Women in Shepherd's Bush, soon renamed Urania Cottage, opens in November, with Dickens in charge of its administration.
1847–1848	Directs and acts in more amateur theatricals.
1848	Thackeray's *Vanity Fair* published. Revolutions throughout Europe. *The Haunted Man*, illustrated by Leech, Stanfield, Frank Stone, and John Tenniel, published December.
1848–1849	Contributes at least 19 articles and reviews to the *Examiner*, probably more.
1849–1850	Thackeray's *Pendennis* published. *David Copperfield*, illustrated by "Phiz," published.
1850	Founds and "conducts" *Household Words*, a weekly journal (30 March 1850–28 May 1859). Wordsworth's *The Prelude, or, Growth of a Poet's Mind*, published. Tennyson's *In Memoriam A.H.H.* published.
1851	His father dies 31 March. Produces and acts in Bulwer-Lytton's comedy, *Not So Bad as We Seem*, to raise funds for the Guild of Literature and Art, founded by Bulwer-Lytton

	and himself. Moves to Tavistock House, Tavistock Square, in November.
1852	*A Child's History of England* (first published in *Household Words*), published.
1852–1853	*Bleak House*, illustrated by "Phiz," published.
1853	Travels in Boulogne with Catherine, the children, and Georgina Hogarth, June to September.
1854	*Hard Times* (first published weekly in *Household Words*), published.
1854–1856	The Crimean War.
1855	Supports the Administrative Reform Association in its criticism of the conduct of the Crimean War.
1855	Directs and acts in a June production of Wilkie Collins's *The Lighthouse* at Tavistock House.
1855–1857	*Little Dorrit*, illustrated by "Phiz," published.
1856	Buys Gad's Hill Place, near Rochester, Kent.
1857	Directs and acts in Wilkie Collins's *The Frozen Deep* to raise money for Douglas Jerrold's family, first in January at Tavistock House, then in August in Manchester, where Ellen Ternan and her sister act in it.
1858	Separates from Catherine in May. From April to November, gives first series of public readings from his works for profit.
1859	Founds and "conducts" a new weekly journal, *All the Year Round*. *A Tale of Two Cities* (first published weekly in *All the Year Round*), illustrated by "Phiz," published. Charles Darwin's *On the Origin of Species* published.
1860	Moves to Gad's Hill Place.
1860–1861	*Great Expectations* (first published weekly in *All the Year Round*) published.
1861–1863	Continues to give public readings.
1863	Thackeray dies 24 December. Despite earlier quarrel (later made up), Dickens writes a generous tribute to him in *Cornhill Magazine* (February 1864).
1864	His mother dies 13 September.
1864–1865	*Our Mutual Friend*, illustrated by Marcus Stone, published.
1865	In the 9 June Staplehurst, Kent, railway accident with Ellen Ternan and her mother, on their return from a visit to France.
1867–1868	Second visit to America to give public readings.

Chronology

1868–1870	Continues to give public readings in London and the provinces.
1870	The first six parts of *The Mystery of Edwin Drood*, illustrated by Luke Fildes and Charles Collins, published.
1870	Dies at Gad's Hill 9 June. Ellen Ternan is among those in the house at the time.
1870	Dean Stanley preaches the sermon at 19 June public funeral service in Westminster Abbey.

Historical and Literary Context

Chapter One

Historical Background

Dickens lived and wrote in the greatest period of social and political reform in English history. His novels straddle the two far-reaching reform bills of 1832 (which he reported in the House of Commons) and 1867, and he knew and highly admired Lord Shaftesbury, inspirer of the factory acts and the most dedicated social reformer of his day. The admiration was mutual: "God had given him," Shaftesbury wrote to Forster, after reading his *Life of Dickens,* "a 'general retainer' for all suffering & oppression; and tho I cannot hold it to be a fact à [propos] writers on human woes that 'he best can paint them, who can feel them most,' I fully believe that it was so with him. He felt what he wrote, and he wrote what he felt; and, as a result, he obtained, &, I am sure, to his heart's joy, a mighty alleviation of tyranny and sorrow."[1] Likewise he knew and admired Edwin Chadwick and Southwood Smith, the leading Victorian sanitary reformers, and Henry Austin, secretary to the new Board of Health, was his brother-in-law. For many years he was the close friend and adviser of the heiress Angela Burdett-Coutts in her many philanthropic schemes, and he planned for her the home for reclaiming prostitutes she set up in Shepherd's Bush.

In the four years, October 1846 to October 1850, that saw the publication of *Dombey and Son* and *David Copperfield,* Dickens was, at the same time, devoting his remarkable energies to these and many other public issues: in two speeches to the Metropolitan Sanitary Association, in the conviction, as he put it in the preface to the cheap edition of *Oliver Twist* (1850), that "[sanitary] Reform must precede all other Social Reforms"; and in articles in the *Examiner* that exposed the appallingly close connection between lack of education and crime, followed by a set of four articles that exposed the horrifying conditions at a "pauper-farm" that had led to the deaths, through cholera, of 180 pauper children. It is hardly surprising that a nonconformist preacher in the 1840s gave him full credit for the reforms that had come about: the "three great social agencies" for reform, he said, were "the London City Mission; the novels of Mr. Dickens; the cholera."[2]

In the middle of this four-year period came the European revolutions of 1848: in France, Germany, Austria-Hungary, Poland, and Italy. As a hater of oppression, Dickens had full sympathy with them. He rejoiced in the proclamation of the Second French Republic, contributed to a fund for the Hungarians, and published in the *Examiner* in 1849 an appeal for funds for the Italian refugees who had fled from Rome after the fall of the Roman Republic. Part of his appeal shows how passionately involved in a political issue he could be: the French invaders, he wrote, had encircled Rome by means of "an act of such stupendous baseness that it will remain an ineffaceable stain upon the honour and the name of France, through all the coming ages of the world."

One inevitable result of the European revolutions was an increase in Chartist activity in England, culminating in the grand Chartist National Convention on Kennington Common of 10 April 1848 (which in fact proved a fiasco). Dickens certainly had some sympathy for the Chartists in their demand for a "People's Charter," but never for the violence of the so-called Physical Force Chartists. In fact, he had little faith in political reform as such. He continually refused to stand for Parliament ("such a club as the Devil has got together," as he once described it to his friend Sir Joseph Paxton);[3] and his only venture into the political arena was at the request of a close friend, Austen Layard, for whose Administrative Reform Committee, attacking the government's handling of the Crimean War, he gave a public speech in June 1855.

But a strong sense of social purpose—to help, above all, the poor, the oppressed, and the outcast—had been an integral part of Dickens's appeal since his earliest writing. Every one of the seven novels before *Copperfield* has some target crying out for reform: the Chancery prisoner in *Pickwick*; the poor law and the London slums in *Oliver Twist*; the Yorkshire schools in *Nicholas Nickleby*; the uncontrolled violence of the London mob and the cynicism or madness of its leaders in *Barnaby Rudge*; the armed bands of the unemployed that terrify Nell and her grandfather in *The Old Curiosity Shop*, and the conditions that led to their eruption; the obsession with money and especially the "almighty dollar" in *Martin Chuzzlewit*; money, again, obsession with class, and a vision of London as vice- and fever-ridden—anticipating *Bleak House*—in *Dombey and Son*.

Copperfield is not without its social criticism; no Dickens novel could be. But, as will be stressed later (see Chapter 10), the explicit criticism is occasional, a throwback to the technique of the earlier novels, never pervasive as it already is in *Dombey and Son*. It is as though, in *Copperfield,* Dickens was taking a rest from the major social issues that had so often haunted his imagination in the past and were to obsess it in the "dark" novels from *Bleak House* onwards. *Copperfield*'s strength is personal and inward: the progress to maturity of the hero, and the careful analysis of often complex human relationships. The comments in his letters on writing it—and particularly from Broadstairs where he finished it—give a sense of relaxation that was rare for him. This inwardness suggests something of the symbolic strength of the Christmas books (a particular link with the last of them, *The Haunted Man* (1848), is suggested later; see Chapter 2), and, through the Christmas books, it suggests the paramount importance to Dickens of childhood.

In *Images of Childhood,* Peter Coveney sees Dickens as the major inheritor of the celebration of childhood by the English romantic poets—by Blake, Coleridge, and Wordsworth in particular.[4] There is no evidence that Dickens had read Blake; but the primary qualities of the children of the novels—the innocence, spontaneity, and sense of wonder of Oliver, Nell, Paul Dombey, David, Pip—are emphatically those of Blake's *Poems of Innocence and Experience*. Although Dickens did not mention Coleridge, whose poems he owned, by name, his attitude to the education and bringing up of children—and especially to the *wrong* kind of "education" in the caricatures of schools he gave us—is profoundly Coleridgean, and never more so than in the claim David Copperfield makes for "the power of observation in numbers of very young children" (2:13). Wordsworth's work he knew well and greatly admired; he owned both Wordsworth's poems and *The Prelude,* and he referred to Wordsworth's "genius" in a diary note in 1838, when he met the poet's younger son.[5] *The Prelude, or, Growth of a Poet's Mind; an Autobiographical Poem* was published in July 1850, when Dickens was writing the last numbers of *David Copperfield,* and David's recovery in the Swiss mountains and valleys from virtual breakdown and the "spots of time" he experiences are strongly Wordsworthian. But it is the claims Wordsworth made in both *The Prelude* and "Intimations of Immortality from Recollections of Early Childhood" for the freedom and instinctive wisdom of the child that Dickens most strikingly inherited, and nowhere more clearly than in the early chapters of *Copperfield.*

The ultimate source for this celebration of the innocence of children, by both the romantic poets and Dickens, is, of course, the New Testament. In *Dickens and Religion* Dennis Walder ably counters the view, put most sharply by Sir Arthur Quiller-Couch in his Cambridge lectures on Dickens, that "to begin with, we must jettison religion."[6] Dickens's Christian convictions as a liberal Protestant in fact permeate all he wrote: his journalism as well as his novels, the Christmas books as well as *The Life of Our Lord,* written for his own children. But what we most remember are the caricatures, the evangelical canters and the Puseyites, both of which types he detested—Stiggins, Chadband, and Mrs. Pardiggle, above all. In *David Copperfield* the Murdstone "religion," essentially Calvinistic, is much more serious: it is not only "austere and wrathful" but it deliberately contradicts the New Testament, its "gloomy theology" making "all children out to be a swarm of little vipers (though there *was* a child once set in the midst of the Disciples)" (4:55). Dickens had originally made both the brutal Creakle and his assistant, Tungay, Calvinists, too—"elect and chosen"—but deleted the derisive paragraph describing them in proof (probably because of its overlap with the Murdstones).[7]

Set against this in-turned, tyrannizing, so-called religion is the social compassion that is Dickens's ideal throughout his writing, and the explicit hallmark of both his weekly journals, *Household Words* and *All the Year Round*. It pervades *David Copperfield*: in the charity with which Daniel Peggotty takes into his home the orphaned little Emily and Ham and the widowed Mrs. Gummidge and in the compassion with which he treats Emily when she is "fallen"; in the care Betsey Trotwood devotes to both David and Mr. Dick and, later, in her help to the Micawbers to emigrate; in the practical dedication Martha Endell shows in searching for little Emily and caring for her until her uncle arrives.

John Forster records that, shortly before beginning *Copperfield*, on the birth of his eighth child on 16 July 1849, Dickens changed the child's name from Oliver Goldsmith to Henry Fielding, "in a kind of homage to the style" of his new work;[8] Fielding's *Tom Jones* is one of the books the young David reads in the attic at Blunderstone (4:55). Dickens's homage was to both Fielding's style and his purpose. With all its autobiographical aim, *David Copperfield*, like *Tom Jones*, is at least a semipicaresque novel; but it also shares the purpose Fielding insisted on in his dedication to Lord Lyttelton: "to recommend goodness and innocence hath been my sincere endeavour in this history." Dickens could have written the same of *Copperfield*, just as he could have claimed, as Fielding did in his first chapter, that what he was providing was "no more than Human Nature."

Chapter Two
The Importance of David Copperfield

Of Dickens's own special involvement with *David Copperfield* there can be no possible doubt. In his preface to the 1867 edition, toward the end of his writing career, he called it his "favourite child": "Of all my books, I like this the best." And, in a letter of 21 October 1850 to his most intimate friend, John Forster, written within a few pages of finishing the final number, he showed how emotionally he had been involved in its writing: "Oh, my dear Forster, if I were to say half of what *Copperfield* makes me feel to-night, how strangely, even to you, I should be turned inside-out! I seem to be sending some part of myself into the Shadowy World" (a phrase that he uses again in both the 1850 and 1867 prefaces).[9]

For *David Copperfield* belongs to that most personal genre of novel, told in the first person (an innovation Forster had encouraged Dickens to try), that German critics, taking as their model Goethe's *Wilhelm Meister* novels (1777–1829), called the bildungsroman: the study of a young man's progress, through struggles, to maturity. And how truthfully Dickens was, in the person of the young David, telling of his own struggles, publication of the first volume of Forster's *Life of Dickens,* in 1872, made clear. The fragment of Dickens's autobiography, written before January 1849 and later destroyed by him, lies only too painfully behind David's experiences in Chapters 11 and 12 of the novel: Jonathan Warren's blacking-warehouse, Hungerford Stairs, Strand, in which the 12-year-old Dickens worked for probably 12–13 months while his father was imprisoned for debt in the Marshalsea, has become Murdstone and Grinby's wine and spirit warehouse, Blackfriars, in which David works as "a little labouring hind" for 6 shillings a week. Many of the other details are the same, and, above all, the intensity of his feelings of permanent deprivation and hopelessness.

The other major incident in the novel that draws on Dickens's own experience is, of course, David's love affair with Dora. But Dickens treated this quite differently. It ends in marriage—even if hardly a satisfactory one—as Dickens's own love affair with Maria Beadnell had emphatically not done. And the irony with which Dickens invested both David and Dora precluded the anguish the young Dickens had undoubtedly felt at losing Maria. The tone of his letter to her (then Mrs. Louis Winter) of 22 February 1855, after she had written to him, reflects a very different emotion from David's feelings, even when beset by obstacles: "But nobody can ever know with what a sad heart I resigned you, or after what struggles and what conflict. My entire devotion to you, and the wasted tenderness of those hard years which I have ever since half loved, half dreaded to recall, made so deep an impression on me." (*Letters* [Nonesuch]:2:629).

The difference in treatment of these two very different autobiographical experiences suggests other strengths of the novel and why it has been, ever since its publication, so universally popular. Above all, it points to Dickens's skill in blending truth and fiction, an "interweaving," as he described it to Forster, of which he was justifiably proud. And secondly, it is evidence of the novel's remarkable variety of tone. Some critics have stressed its ease and confidence, its light irony, the "charm" that so impressed Thackeray (in a letter to Mrs. Brookfield), and the absence of any crisis in the writing, such as had beset *Dombey and Son* only 18 months before. Sylvère Monod, for example, in *Dickens the Novelist*, entitles the section on *David Copperfield*, "At the Top."[10] Others have stressed the opposite: the intensity of David's suffering at the hands of the Murdstones and on the Dover Road; the pathos of the deaths of his mother and Dora; the disaster of the storm, which brings the deaths of Steerforth and Ham. More personally, David's "one happiness I have missed in life, and one friend and companion I have never made," becomes an index, for some commentators, to a generally pervasive sadness.

Both tones are unquestionably there, as they are in all the most characteristic Dickens works. But the novel embraces many more: the comedy stretches from the more than life-size, exuberantly liberating Micawbers to the enchanting impracticalities of Dora's housekeeping, and the sense of corruption or straightforward villainy from Miss Mowcher's first appearance (her strongly suggested corruption there was later deliberately changed by Dickens when his model for the dwarf threatened legal action) to the malignant Uriah Heep. The novel contains in fact a surprising amount of sexual experience, overt and covert: besides the central little Emily story, of which Dickens was extremely proud, there is Martha, the prostitute; the sexually threatening Heep; the "January-May" marriage of the Strongs and Annie Strong's relationship with Jack Maldon; and the powerfully observed study of sexual frustration in Mrs. Steerforth's companion, Rosa Dartle, a study not equaled in intensity until years later in the story of Miss Wade, "the history of a self-tormentor," in *Little Dorrit*. Even the indomitable Betsey Trotwood has her own dark history of sexual betrayal.

As in all bildungsromanen, all these characters have some connection with David himself, and to suggest that interconnectedness, with its full implications, was one of the triumphant achievements of the maturing Dickens. But in a novel as personal as *David Copperfield* (*Great Expectations* was his only other bildungsroman), truthfulness to memory had to take precedence over the novelist's other arts; in important ways, *Copperfield* is a novel of memory, Dickens's *A la recherche du temps perdu*. In these middle years of his writing life (he was not quite 37 when he began *Copperfield*), Dickens was acutely aware of his past and of the necessity of coming to terms with it. The fragment of autobiography already discussed is, of course, the chief evidence for his consciousness of that necessity. But he was intensely interested in the force and value of memory itself. In the last of his Christmas books, *The Haunted Man* (December 1848), written shortly before he began *Copperfield,* he showed the wrong and suffer-ing caused by the taking away of memory: the book's epitaph is "Lord, keep my memory green!" In Chapter 2 of *Copperfield,* he not only created the child's-eye vision of the boy David by a succession of precise, sensuously experienced memories, but he wrote a paean to the powers of close observation in very young children and to his own "strong memory" of his childhood. The pattern is completed when, as a successful novelist at the end of *Copperfield,* David himself writes novels based on his own memories.

Memory leads, of course, to realism; there can be no doubt of the intense reality of David's experiences, particularly in the early chapters of the novel. But Dickens again and again insisted on fancy or imagination as an essential ingredient of the novelist's art. There is, as in almost all of Dickens's novels, plenty of grotesque fancy in *David Copperfield,* ranging from Mr. Dick and the obtrusive King Charles's head (changed in proof from the bull in a china shop) to Mr. Barkis secreting his money box under his bed. But more important, the realism combines with many features of the fairy tale, as will be shown in Chapter 11.

Chapter Three
Critical Reception

There was a remarkable unanimity in the immediate response to *David Copperfield,* among other novelists as well as critics. Thackeray's enthusiasm, in a letter of 4 May 1849 to his friend Mrs. Brookfield—when the first number (Chapters 1–3) had just appeared—is justly famous: "O it is charming. Bravo Dickens. It has some of his very prettiest touches—those inimitable Dickens touches w^h make such a great man of him." And shortly afterwards, to her husband: "Get David Copperfield: by Jingo it's beautiful—it beats the yellow chap [his own *Pendennis*] of this month hollow." Charlotte Brontë, after praising it to her publisher as "very good—admirable in some parts," shrewdly discriminated between it and her own *Jane Eyre* (1847), with which her publisher had found an "affinity"): "It has [an affinity], now and then—only what an advantage has Dickens in his varied knowledge of men and things!" Among other writers, it was the special favorite of Harriet Martineau, who described it as "prodigiously fine."[11]

John Forster, Dickens's closest friend, devoted five pages of his *Life of Dickens* to the novel. Authoritative on the autobiographical content and on the living models Dickens drew on (more expectedly, perhaps, than in any other novel), his general appraisal is that of numerous critics at the time: "He has nowhere given such variety of play to his invention, and the book is unapproached among his writings for its completeness of effect and uniform pleasantness of tone" (553).

Variety of incident, richness of invention, structural skill, and tonal harmony are stressed again and again in contemporary reviews. One of the best-known and longest of them, David Masson's "*Pendennis* and *Copperfield:* Thackeray and Dickens" (*North British Review,* May 1851), draws a comparison between the two novels, which were published in monthly numbers almost simultaneously; such a comparison became an obvious attraction for many other critics, too. Most of the distinctions Masson makes have now long been accepted: in style and language, "Thackeray is the more terse and idiomatic . . . Dickens the more diffuse and luxuriant"; in social description, Thackeray exhibits "a knowingness . . . a worldly shrewdness and sagacity"; in Dickens we do not see that "close-grained solidity of view" but, instead, when his feelings are moved, the "concentration and melody . . . of an essentially susceptible and poetic nature." It was precisely this that Forster claims in an unsigned review of Dickens's next novel, *Bleak House,* in the *Examiner* (October 1853): "Novels as Mr. Dickens writes them rise to the dignity of poems." This observation points toward much modern and symbolist criticism of Dickens, and it goes back to the best-known—and then most challenging—of Masson's contrasts: between Thackeray as a "realist" and Dickens as an "idealist," above all, in the creation of character. "It is nonsense," writes Masson,

> to say of [Dickens's] characters generally . . . that they are life-like. They are nothing of the kind. . . . Not only are his serious or tragic creations . . . persons of romance; but even his comic or satiric portraitures do not come within the strict bounds of the real. There never was a real Mr. Pickwick, a real Sam Weller, a real Mrs. Nickleby, a real Quilp, a real Micawber, a real Uriah Heep, or a real Toots, in the same accurate sense that there has been or might be a real Major Pendennis, a real Captain Costigan, a real Becky, a real Sir Pitt Crawley, and a real Mr. Foker.

Masson ends this central section of his article by invoking two of the indisputably great writers, and by putting both firmly on Dickens's side: "The characters of Shakespeare are not, in any common sense, life-like"; and, "Art is called Art, says Goethe, precisely because it is *not* Nature."

Samuel Phillips, in the *Times* (11 June 1851), also compares *Copperfield* and *Pendennis* and also comes down finally and strongly on Dickens's side, because it is "the whole world rather than a bit of it" that Dickens gives; because the tone of *Copperfield* is "as a whole, light-hearted and hopeful, the other dolorous, and depressing"; and also because "the expressed morality" (particularly the lessons of faith in Mr. Peggotty and resignation in Ham) counts for more than Thackeray's critical experiments on "a world of salamanders, fireproof." "The epic is greater than the satire."

Dickens himself would have rejoiced in this recognition of his "expressed morality," and particularly of the powers of simplicity, ruggedness, and tenderness he had given to the inhabitants of the Yarmouth boat. Of all the homes in *David Copperfield*, good and bad, the boat most reflects his ideal; one sentence in an unsigned review in *Fraser's* magazine (December 1859) finds the chief reason for his widespread popularity in "his deep reverence for the household sanctities, his enthusiastic worship of the household gods."

The reviewer here clearly had in mind Dickens's new weekly journal, *Household Words*—whose first number had appeared in May 1850, seven months before the conclusion of *Copperfield*—and the aims its "Conductor," as Dickens called himself, had set for it. Some of those aims chime in exactly with the values represented by Mr. Peggotty and his family: the spreading of "Household tenderness," or wholesome humor and fancy, of belief in the sanctities of the home. His other main aim was just as important: "the raising up of those that are down, and the general improvement of our social condition," as he put it to Mrs. Gaskell on 31 January 1850. "All social evils, and all home affections and associations," he told Mrs. Howitt three weeks later, "I am particularly anxious to deal with, well" (*Letters* 6:22, 41).

There are, in fact, few social evils in *Copperfield*, and no sense of what Carlyle had called, in *Chartism* (1840), the "Condition-of-England question." The evils that cause the suffering are personal: the perverse, aggressive Calvinism of the Murdstones; the reckless and sensual irresponsibility of Steerforth, made more dangerous by his charm; the treachery of Littimer; the malignant hypocrisy of Uriah Heep. One "social evil" Dickens does portray is, of course, prostitution; but Martha, aside from her symbolic use in dogging little Emily and her ultimate part in the plot, is an entirely stereotyped picture, infinitely less individual than some of the girls Dickens had to deal with in Miss Burdett-Coutts's Home for Homeless Women. Another is the system of middle-class "education" immortalized in Mr. Creakle and Salem House—and used by Matthew Arnold 30 years later as a stick with which to beat the philistines.[12] The nearest to social evils, apart from these, are the hidebound corruption of Doctors' Commons, represented by the vain Mr. Spenlow and his ineffectual partner, Mr. Jorkins; and the absurdity of the separate prison system, governed by the likes of Creakle, shown as totally deceived by the "two interesting penitents," Heep and Littimer. But the satirical chapters dealing with both institutions are curiously irrelevant both to the plot and to the dominant tones of the rest of the novel.

It is in his next novel, *Bleak House* (1852–53)—the first of the "dark period" novels, which Dickens began to write a year after finishing *Copperfield*—that the social evils interconnect to form an entire, and entirely diseased, world. There he anatomized the whole of contemporary society: Chancery abuse, financial corruption, political misgovernment, and the hideousness and threat to health of the London slums; the contrast of tone with *Copperfield* is absolute. Inevitably, then, for many critics, *Bleak House* became a watershed. For those for whom Dickens's true genius lay in comedy and pathos and, as the *Fraser's* magazine reviewer of *Copperfield* put it, in his "all-pervading charity," the sacrifice of these gifts for the dark social criticism and ferocious satire of *Bleak House* was anathema. For those who shared Dickens's fervent belief that the serious novelist must write with an object, that, writing in the mid-nineteenth century, he must at least lay bare the "Condition-of-England question," *David Copperfield* represents the end of a happier era and *Bleak House* is the first of the greatest novels.

But for the reading public at large, *David Copperfield* has remained one of Dickens's best-loved novels. The immense success of his public reading of it (in six chapters, blending David's love affair with Dora and their marriage with the story of Mr. Peggotty, little Emily, and Steerforth, and culminating in the storm), first given in October 1861, undoubtedly played its part in this; like the novel itself, it was Dickens's own favorite reading. The suspicion—not confirmed until the first volume of Forster's *Life* in 1872—that, as Forster puts it, "underneath the fiction lay something of the author's life" also kept a special interest alive. Only two months before Dickens's death, Sir Arthur Helps, clerk to the Privy Council, advising Queen Victoria on her meeting with Dickens at Buckingham Palace on 9 March 1870, wrote to her: "One of his best works is *David Copperfield:* and it is supposed that it gives or at least gives a hint of the narrative of the author's early life."

Forster's publication of the autobiographical fragment, with its revelation of Dickens's sufferings as a 12-year-old boy, has had a profound effect on all twentieth-century Dickens criticism and, inevitably, has sharpened interest in *David Copperfield* itself. For Edmund Wilson, whose essay on Dickens, "The Two Scrooges," has had an all-pervasive influence over the last 50 years, the experience of the blacking-warehouse by the young boy was a traumatic injury; to him, many elements in Dickens's whole creative life were an attempt to come to terms with it.[13] Foremost among these elements are the early child's-eye visions of Oliver Twist, Paul Dombey, and David: innocent, observant, sensitive, formidably truthful and independent, but all unjustly suffering in different ways. Oliver remains a boy throughout his novel; Paul dies in childhood; only in *David Copperfield* (followed by Pip in *Great Expectations*) do we see the child grow up. And much twentieth-century criticism has found the adult David and, with him, the larger last part of the novel, disappointing after the wonderful early chapters. Wilson himself gives the highest praise to the early part: "Dickens strikes an enchanting vein which he never quite found before and which he was never to find again" (43). An excellent essay by John Jones adjudicates sharply between the two parts of the novel and, it seems to me, is equally persuasive on both.[14] No other critic that I know has described the young David so well: "the tough little life always pressing up from beneath the buffeting, with its unquenchable curiosity and self-concern, with its ultimate pertness which is almost blitheness" (135). But, he goes on, using the image of the ship that Dickens had used to Forster a day or two before finishing the novel ("I am within three pages of the shore"), after the Betsey Trotwood–Murdstone explosion in Dover, the novel "shudders helplessly, motionless like a sailing ship in irons" (134). After this, Jones sees "a weakened narrative thrust" and a prose that lacks the life of the early chapters, with David's sojourn in Switzerland as the weakest part. But Jones continues the sailing-ship image in discussing the text after the Dover explosion; this analysis seems to me more open to doubt. "Then it pays away, gradually, from the eye of the wind, and its sails fill upon a new tack which it holds to the end; and the end is a completed portrait of the artist as a young man" (136). There are indeed plenty of new tacks in a novel that abounds with varied plots and incidents, and Dickens showed great skill in relating them all to David, either as participant or observer. But the "portrait of the artist" we are given is, frankly, disappointing: "It is not my purpose, in this record, though in all other essentials it is my written memory, to pursue the history of my own fictions. They express themselves, and I leave them to themselves" (48:690).

Disappointment with the post–Dover Road David is shared by many twentieth-century critics; the new picture we are given includes, of course, the changes in David's ambience. Creakle and Salem House are, as Matthew Arnold said, "immortal"; Dr. Strong's school at Canterbury is clearly an excellent institution, but, as described, its feet are firmly on the ground. Similarly with David's new home: Mr. Wickfield's house has all the ordered picturesqueness that the Victorians made into an ideal; but it totally lacks the sharp, odd, individual detail that makes both the Rookery and the Yarmouth boat so compellingly and attractively real. The order at Mr. Wickfield's is, of course, supplied by Agnes, the "real heroine" of the novel, as Dickens describes her in one of the memorandum notes that he made for planning his novels (now bound up with the manuscripts in the Forster Collection, Victoria and Albert Museum); but almost all critics over the last 50 years and more have found her an embarrassment. It is not only that she is intensely idealized, but that the ideal, the "stained glass window in a church" (David's response on first seeing her [15:223]), is a peculiarly lifeless one. George Orwell derides her as "the real legless angel of Victorian romance," and most critics have contrasted her unfavorably with David's charming, sexually provoking, if hopelessly impractical, "child-wife" Dora. Michael Slater, in *Dickens and Women*, is surely right to claim that the shade of Mary Hogarth, Catherine's younger sister who had died in his arms in 1837, aged 17, lies behind Agnes (as behind many of his idealized young heroines), inhibiting any trace of either comedy or sexual attractiveness; while behind Dora, in her loveliness, artless innocence, affection, and sexual attraction, lie the remembered charms of Maria Beadnell, comically presented—the darker elements of Dickens's anguish, when the love affair broke down, now forgiven.[15]

But the major tack that keeps *David Copperfield* sailing vigorously to the end is the comic life of the Micawbers; all critics are agreed on their major contribution to the novel. Micawber's ancestry in John Dickens gives us the early scenes of pecuniary embarrassment—debts, unpaid bills not taken up, employment always around the corner—that Dickens remembered only too well from his boyhood; here again, the comedy both frees and forgives. The early chapters, too, give us the Micawbers as David's much-needed surrogate parents. But Micawber has a more important ancestry, too. In the Dickens canon he stands with Sam Weller, Sairey Gamp, and Mr. Pecksniff as a comic, self-creating voice, but beyond them, with Falstaff himself. In his own verbal grandiloquence and protean volatility, he constantly parodies the romanticism of both David and Steerforth, and his comic pretentiousness burlesques David's more serious social pretensions; like Falstaff, he constantly subverts. The great scene near the end, in which he exposes Heep (Chapter 52), in fact doubles his power: he is here both theatrical stage manager and parodist of the melodrama he has himself created.

Thackeray may have written to David Masson—thanking him for his review of *Pendennis* and *Copperfield*—that Dickens, in his art, did not represent nature duly: "For instance Micawber appears to me an exaggeration of a man, as his name is of a name. It is delightful and makes me laugh: but he is no more a real man than my friend Punch is: and in so far I protest against him."[16] But Dickens's vast public has come down strongly on the side of his art and the imagination that fueled it; Micawber is, of course, "an exaggeration of a man," but a deliberately comic exaggeration, with both a function and a buoyancy that are essential to the liberating effect of the whole novel.

One great contemporary novelist who paid Dickens the sincerest compliment of taking him as a model was Tolstoy. In later life he proclaimed Dickens as his favorite writer and *David Copperfield* as his favorite novel. Dickens's portrait hung in his study. A. N. Wilson, in his recent biography of Tolstoy, shows how what he calls "Copperfield-mania" gripped the Russians, including Tolstoy, on the novel's almost immediate translation, and how much Tolstoy modeled his first publication, *Childhood* (1852), on *Copperfield*, above all, in portraying the childhood memories of a young boy, an idealized hero worship that, as Wilson says, corresponds exactly with David's feelings for Steerforth (the desire to *be* Steerforth), and the crisis—the death of the young narrator's mother.

Several contemporary critics may have found both Agnes and the later David disappointing, but others have recognized quintessential Dickensian qualities and concerns in the novel as a whole. Harry Stone, for instance, devotes much the longest chapter of his book, *Dickens and the Invisible World*, to *David Copperfield*, and he shows convincingly how Dickens's conscious or subconscious belief in the powers of fantasy and enchantment deepen the everyday concerns of the novel (see Chapter 11). Allan Grant, in *A Preface to Dickens*, sees "the everyday and the domestic" as similarly transformed into "great art"; but the transforming agency, for him, is a deliberate following of Wordsworth's prescription for his own poetry, as set out in his Preface to the Lyrical Ballads: "to choose incidents and situations from common life, and to relate . . . them . . . in a selection of language really used by men, and, at the same time to throw over them a certain colouring of imagination."[17] For the language of one group of his characters, Mr. Peggotty and his family, rooted in common life as they are, Dickens took great pains to reproduce the Suffolk dialect. And, as Grant rightly stresses, many of the novel's metaphors and similes are drawn from common experience.

Dickens's satire of the Murdstones' harsh and gloomy Calvinism—of the *wrong* kind of religion—is, as we would expect, stressed by Dennis Walder in his *Dickens and Religion;* but he also draws attention to religious overtones throughout the novel and to language clearly rooted in the Bible. David's recurrent sense of an "old unhappy loss or want of something" is the nineteenth-century romantic's longing for self-fulfillment, and as virtually repeated in 1854 by Dickens himself to Forster, it shows that the autobiography in *David Copperfield* is much more private and intimate than a repetition of actual events: "Why is it, that as with poor David, a sense comes always crushing on me now, when I fall into low spirits, as of one happiness I have missed in life, and of one friend and companion I have never made?" (Forster, 629). But the deprivation David records has, as Walder points out, ultimate religious overtones, and Agnes, recognized finally as the filler of his void, always "pointing upward" (64:877), is described in explicit New Testament language: "My wife; my love of whom was founded on a rock!" (62:864).

Michael Allen, in a recent book, *Charles Dickens' Childhood,* has produced important new documentary evidence to show that the 12-year-old Dickens worked in the blacking-warehouse not for 4–6 months, as was previously assumed by many, but for 12–13 months.[18] Such a discovery increases manyfold the traumatic effect these months, apparently eternal, must have had on a young and sensitive boy. The effect on his life and work, when the period was thought to be six months or less, was acutely analyzed by Edmund Wilson in "The Two Scrooges." The effect of the full year's horror on *David Copperfield* was clearly crucial.

A Reading

My Magnificent Order at the Public-house (Chapter 11) by H. K. Browne.
Reproduced by permission of Oxford University Press.

Chapter Four

The Child's-Eye Vision

On completing the writing of Chapter 2 of *David Copperfield* ("I Observe"), Dickens rejected the latest of many titles he was trying out, "The Copperfield Survey of the World as It Rolled," and gave the novel its final title, *The Personal History of David Copperfield*. The change underscored his decision to write the whole novel in the first person, to "interweave," as he put it to Forster, the facts of his own childhood with fiction (or fancy), and, above all, to give the reader what Edmund Wilson has well called "an idealized version of the loves and fears and wonders of childhood." It is the intensity of that "version" (or child's-eye vision) that makes the first 14 chapters of the novel, culminating in Betsey Trotwood's defeat of the Murdstones, some of the most memorable writing in Dickens.

Two things stand out in the early chapters: truthfulness, both in the experiences re-created and in David's emotional response to them; and the range and variety of tone conjured up by the mature Dickens in the telling of childhood experience. Many critics have commented on the ease and confidence that envelop the novel as a whole, and to some extent, these qualities, as well as a half-comic irony, play their part in softening the extremes of feeling in the early chapters. But what we most remember are the extremes: the intensity of David's love for his mother; the elysium of his childhood romance with little Emily; his total trust in Peggotty and, on the other side, his jealousy of Murdstone; his anguish at Murdstone's coldness and heartlessness, both on his mother's behalf and his own; his terrors, both of Murdstone's violence and of the nightmare of the journey to Dover; and the degradation he so keenly feels as "a labouring hind" at Murdstone and Grinby's. Dickens caught a very real childhood belief: the conviction that an experience, whether delightful or painful, will last forever, a strong sense of the permanency of bliss or anguish.

But what Dickens caught best in the opening number (Chapters 1–3) is a child's sense of wonder, beautifully recorded in David's memories of his home at Blunderstone. Touch, sight, and smell are the three senses most vividly evoked in the child David, and all are communicated with the immediacy that belongs to a child. Almost David's first experience is the "touch of Peggotty's forefinger as she used to hold it out to me, and of its being roughened by needlework, like a pocket nutmeg-grater" (2:13). This "may be fancy," may be remembrance, says Dickens, and it leads him to make a case for both the memory and the power of observation of very young children. And the observation gives total authenticity to David's next recorded experiences: the "fowls that look terribly tall to me, walking about in a menacing and ferocious manner" (the child's scale of dimensions); and the vivid sense of smell from the dark storeroom, which he runs past, frightened, at night, "the smell of soap, pickles, pepper, candles, and coffee, all at one whiff" (2:14).

But it is essential to the early part of the novel that Blunderstone begin as paradise to the young David. Dickens skillfully suggested this by several devices: the deliberate use of hyperbole (David remembers the garden, "where the fruit clusters on the trees, riper and richer than fruit has ever been since, in any other garden" [2:15]); and the use of the present tense to suggest a permanent state of idyllic bliss ("A great wind rises, and the summer is gone in a moment. We are playing in the winter twilight, dancing about the parlour" [15:15–16]). Any danger of sentimentality here is delicately controlled by the comedy: the church service, the crocodile book, the innocent, understandable flytings of David's mother and Peggotty.

Wonder predominates in the next chapter, too, and is at its peak in David's delight in Mr. Peggotty's boat-house, with the individual, colorful, almost surreal details of the pictures inside stamped indelibly on the child's memory: "Abraham in red going to sacrifice Isaac in blue, and Daniel in yellow cast into a den of green lions" (3:30). But the paradisal element here is, of course, his love for "little Em'ly" and her love for him, framed in a time scale given us not by David as a child but by the mature Dickens looking nostalgically back: "The days sported by us, as if Time had not grown up himself yet, but were a child too, and always at play" (3:37). This follows the long passage, inserted by Dickens after finishing his first draft of the number, that looks not back but forward, the passage in which Emily says she would like to be "a lady," to help Mr. Peggotty and Ham, and that ends, after she has sprung forward apparently "to her destruction" in the deep sea: "There has been a time since . . . when I have asked myself the question, would it have been better for little Em'ly to have had the waters close above her head that morning in my sight; and when I have answered Yes, it would have been" (3:36–37).

Dickens was doing much more than playing with the time scale, he was pointing forward to a central event in the novel, Steerforth's seduction of Emily with the specious promise to make her a lady. This early passage is impressive as an example of Dickens's close control of the structure of *David Copperfield* throughout, but it also points to the flexibility in the use of time that the employment of the single person as narrator gave him. This flexibility includes switches from the past to the present tense to achieve the immediacy of the early chapters; four chapters entitled "Retrospect" interspersed through the novel; and the use of Wordsworthian "spots of time" in Chapter 58, "Absence," to illuminate David's recovery. A further technique ends the chapter (and the number). David returns to his home to find his new stepfather, Mr. Murdstone, in control. Emblems are used to underline the changes to come: the shrubs outside his window are now "drooping their heads in the cold" and the empty dog kennel is "filled up with a great dog—deep-mouthed and black-haired like Him—and he was very angry at the sight of me, and sprang out to get at me" (3:43).

If the first number suggests paradise—or at any rate, glimpses of paradise—Chapter 4 ("I fall into Disgrace") records, for a sensitive, affectionate boy, more than glimpses of purgatory. This analogue seems justified by Dickens's stress on "the Murdstone religion, which was austere and wrathful," and on the Murdstones' "gloomy theology," which "made all children out to be a swarm of little vipers" (55), as well as by his description of "firmness," the Murdstones' "grand quality," in phrases clearly intended to parody the Creed: David's mother "might be firm, and must be; but only in bearing [the Murdstones'] firmness, and firmly believing there was no other firmness upon earth" (49). Coldness and iron-heartedness have now totally replaced the spontaneous love of David's old home. David himself will be the first victim; his mother, Dickens makes clear by a succession of hints, will not survive the Murdstone tyranny.

There is some grim comedy: the description of Miss Murdstone and her steel fetters and rivets ("I had never, at that time, seen such a metallic lady altogether as Miss Murdstone was" [4:48]); her opening words to David: "Generally speaking . . . I don't like boys. How d'ye do, boy?" (4:48); and the appalling sum set for David by Mr. Murdstone: "'If I go into a cheesemonger's shop, and buy five thousand double-Gloucester cheeses at fourpence-halfpenny each, present payment'—at which I see Miss Murdstone secretly overjoyed" (4:54–55). But the lessons, for which Dickens goes again into the present tense ("Let me remember how it used to be, and bring one morning back again" [4:53]), culminate in the act of violence that virtually ends the Murdstone-David relationship. The violence itself is quickly over: Murdstone's caning of David and David's biting through his hand. David's five-day imprisonment in his room ("Child's remembrance of the latter" is underlined in Dickens's memorandum for the chapter) is his real purgatory, and his fears and anguish are described with an unerring insight into a terrified and lonely child's mind: the five days that seem like five years; the life of the house that goes on without him; and, above all, the terrible feeling of guilt. "Whether it was a criminal act that I had committed? Whether I should be taken into custody, and sent to prison? Whether I was at all in danger of being hanged?" (4:59).

But the chapter does offer two consolations to David: the discovery of his father's "small collection of books," which he reads omnivorously—Smollett, Fielding, Goldsmith, Defoe, besides *Don Quixote*, the *Arabian Nights*, and the *Tales of the Genii*—taken, of course, from Dickens's own autobiographical fragment ("every word," says Forster, "had been written down as fact, some years before it found its way into *David Copperfield*" [Forster, 1:6]); and the beautifully described visit of Peggotty to his prison, ending with their both kissing the keyhole.

After the anguish and intensity of most of that chapter, the dominant tone of the next three—David's being sent away to school, Mr. Mell's looking after him, and his "First Half" at Salem House—mingles a boy's fears and loneliness with a relatively new and growing confidence. Incidents like his being robbed by the waiter are given a new self-protective irony. The terrible placard Murdstone has ordered he should wear ("Take care of him. He bites") causes him terrors for when the other boys return—and how perceptively Dickens conjures up a boy's terrors of humiliation and mockery!—but is quickly reduced to a game by the amiable Traddles. His fears from the other boys—again, acutely described—are soon ended by Steerforth's protection. Salem House itself, based on Wellington House Academy—the school in Hampstead Road Dickens had himself been sent to, after release from Warren's blacking-warehouse—is realized with all the immediacy of these early chapters: its smells ("There is a strange unwholesome smell upon the room, like mildewed corduroys, sweet apples wanting air, and rotten books" [5:77–78]); the playground door carved with boys' names, each of whom causes him anticipatory dread; and, above all, the ignorant and sadistic headmaster, Mr. Creakle, who delights particularly in caning "chubby" boys, and his assistant, the coarse, bullying, wooden-legged Tungay. As a pair, they are unforgettably grotesque, with Tungay acting as interpreter for the virtually voiceless Creakle: "'I'll tell you what I am,' whispered Mr. Creakle, letting [my ear] go at last, with a screw at parting that brought the water into my eyes, 'I'm a Tartar.' 'A Tartar,' said the man with the wooden leg. 'When I say I'll do a thing, I do it,' said Mr. Creakle; 'and when I say I will have a thing done, I will have it done.' '—Will have a thing done, I will have it done,' repeated the man with the wooden leg." (6:82)

But the new note of confidence comes from the two friends David makes in the school, quite different as they are, James Steerforth and Tommy Traddles. David's friendship with the much older Steerforth is at once a perceptive study in hero worship and a fine study in irony. Steerforth is a "great scholar . . . very good-looking," of engaging manners, and "a person of great power" in David's eyes; he promises to take care of his young friend (his later nicknaming David "Daisy" stresses the masculine-feminine in such a relationship, or rather, the fact that Steerforth sees it as that). With no father to remember except the appalling Murdstone, David gives Steerforth all the admiration and love of which his affectionate nature is capable. But the irony begins at once. David and the other boys may set Steerforth on a pedestal, but the cracks soon appear. His confiscation and spending of David's money hardly go with a noble, disinterested nature, any more than his allowing Traddles to suffer for his own transgression in church. And on both occasions, Dickens makes it clear that the young David knows instinctively that Steerforth is in the wrong. These may be minor matters. But Steerforth's treatment of Mr. Mell in front of Creakle and the whole school, which results in Mell's dismissal (Chapter 7), is anything but minor. It anticipates the darker side of Steerforth's character—his arrogance and cruelty. It also shows that Traddles, caned for being "discovered in tears, instead of cheers" on Mr. Mell's behalf, has a strong sense of fairness. But above all, it exposes unerringly a child's sense of guilt in David. He may, with the other boys, have "exalted Steerforth to the skies"; but he knows only too well that it was he who had told Steerforth of Mr. Mell's mother living in an almshouse, and he now suffers for it: "But I must say that when I was going on with a story in the dark that night, Mr. Mell's old flute seemed more than once to sound mournfully in my ears; and that when at last Steerforth was tired, and I lay down in my bed, I fancied it playing so sorrowfully somewhere, that I was quite wretched" (7:101).

Such is the way in which Dickens registered moral judgments: Mr. Mell's old flute tells strongly against Steerforth's insensitiveness; but, ironically, it is the young David who suffers and the child's eye that sees through to the truth.

A delicate differentiation of tones plays its part in David's and Steerforth's responses to Mr. Peggotty and Ham when they visit David toward the end of Chapter 7. David's enthusiasm is wholly spontaneous, his mixture of crying and laughing the right emotional response of an excited young boy. Steerforth's is, of course, more mature, but with the conscious (and totally successful) intent to charm, there is more than a hint of patronage too: "'You never saw such a good house, Steerforth. It's made out of a boat,' says David. 'Made out of a boat, is it?' said Steerforth. 'It's the right sort of a house for such a thorough-built boatman.'" And, to Mr. Peggotty's "I thankee, sir, I thankee! I do my endeavours in my line of life, sir," Steerforth replies, "The best of men can do no more, Mr. Peggotty." Adds the spellbound David, "He had got his name already" (7:104–5).

Chapter 8 ("My Holidays. Especially one Happy Afternoon") is really a series of vignettes, happy, nostalgic, interspersed with the Murdstones' dislike and rejection of the young David. It is as though the Rookery were now divided into two: the home, emblem for Dickens of all good, the loved abode of David's mother, Peggotty, and David himself; and its parody, the gloom-laden *habitat* of the Murdstones. But the sense of an ending gathering over the real home is strongly conjured up; here, of course, it is the mature Dickens speaking, in a sense doing the memorizing for David: "We were very happy; and that evening, as the last of its race, and destined evermore to close that volume of my life, will never pass out of my memory" (8:115).

The energy in the chapter—negative energy—is given to the vindictive Murdstones. Miss Murdstone's horror at David's taking up his baby brother, followed by her fury at David's mother saying that the baby's and David's eyes are alike, symbolizes the real ejection of David from the home. His enforced presence, at Murdstone's sufferance, turns the value of the shared hearth into a mockery. It exists momentarily again, but only when Dickens has made it clear, at the end of the chapter, that it is too late: "So I lost her. So I saw her afterwards, in my sleep at school—a silent presence near my bed—looking at me with the same intent face—holding up her baby in her arms" (8:121).

Sentimentality here is held at bay by a striking verbal economy. In the next chapter, the last of the number, the emotion over the death of David's mother, by now fully prepared for, and her funeral is controlled by the equally striking and unexpected presence of delicate humor. A letter Dickens wrote to his friend Mark Lemon on 25 June 1849, soon after finishing the chapter, shows indeed how far he could distance himself from a major grief of the novel, without diminishing the pathos in the writing in the slightest: "Get a clean pocket-handkerchief ready for the close of 'Copperfield' No. 3; 'simple and quiet, but very natural and touching.'—*Evening Bore*."[19]

David's response when Mrs. Creakle tells him his mother is very ill and he divines the truth at once is conveyed with impressive imaginative truthfulness (this, after all, was not part of the autobiographical fragment): "A mist rose between Mrs. Creakle and me, and her figure seemed to move in it for an instant."

What follows shows Dickens's penetration into a child's mind at its keenest and boldest. David cries and cries; his grief is totally sincere. Then "I . . . looked into the glass to see how red my eyes were, and how sorrowful my face." "I am sensible of having felt that a dignity attached to me among the rest of the boys, and that I was important in my affliction." In the playground he feels "distinguished, and looked more melancholy, and walked slower"; when the boys speak to him, "I felt it rather good in myself not to be proud to any of them, and to take exactly the same notice of them all, as before" (9:123–24).

This has the ring of absolute truth: Dickens writing from the inside. The scene that follows, at the home of jovial Mr. Omer, the undertaker, has a different kind of humor, on the edge of the grotesque; but it is held sharply in focus by a boy's observation. "I remark this, because I remark everything that happens," as David says later in the chapter. And, again, the humor does not destroy the pathos; if anything, as in Shakespeare—and one thinks inevitably of the grave-diggers in *Hamlet*—it increases the pathos. Sounds are important to David now. He knows instinctively that the "RAT-tat-tat, RAT-tat-tat, RAT-tat-tat" from across the yard comes from the hammering on his mother's coffin; he records, without comment (and the juxtaposition of tones bites deep here), the cheerfulness of the Omer family in front of him: "'You are such a comfortable man, you see,' said Minnie. 'You take things so easy.' 'No use taking 'em otherwise, my dear,' said Mr. Omer. 'No, indeed,' returned his daughter. 'We are all pretty gay here, thank Heaven! Ain't we, father?' 'I hope so, my dear,' said Mr. Omer." Then the more macabre memories of David's long-dead father: "'I have been acquainted with you a long time, my young friend.' 'Have you, Sir?' 'All your life,' said Mr. Omer. 'I may say before it. I knew your father before you. He was five foot nine and a half and he lays in five and twen-ty foot of ground.' RAT-tat-tat, RAT-tat-tat, RAT-tat-tat, across the yard" (9:125–26).

The funeral is described in the present tense, the details, like Mr. Chillip's kindness to David, etched in with the sharpness of memory; but the description is framed by Peggotty's narration to David of his mother's last days. In the final two paragraphs of the chapter Dickens switched time schemes yet again, so that the image of David's mother we are left with is an all-important one for the rest of the novel: "The young mother of my earliest impressions, who had been used to wind her bright curls round and round her finger, and to dance with me at twilight in the parlour" (9:133).

But the next number, beginning with Chapter 10 ("I become Neglected, and am Provided for"), is all-important in another way. It is here that Dickens made most use of the autobiographical fragment he had shown to Forster and at the same time had to meet the challenge of controlling the pervasive temptation to self-pity. His first memorandum note, "what I know so well," said a great deal. But a letter to

Forster of 10 July 1849, when he was still writing the number, shows how the mature writer had already found a method of distancing himself from over-absorption in the sufferings of his young self: "I really think I have done it ingeniously, and with a very complicated interweaving of truth and fiction. Vous verrez." And he went on: "I am getting on like a house afire in point of health, and ditto ditto in point of number" (*Letters* 5:569). The confidence was totally justified. The whole chapter, the visit to Yarmouth that is the prelude to the hell of Murdstone and Grinby's warehouse, is a mixture of comedy and pathos that most appealed to Dickens himself—and certainly to his readers. There is in fact more comedy than pathos; but the effect is to put the shock of the plans for David's "employment," described in the last few pages, into sharper and grimmer focus.

After quickly establishing David's new neglect, the first part of the chapter is almost all comedy: Barkis's wooing of Peggotty, with David as naive go-between; their marriage, with David and little Emily as the only witnesses; the affectionately ironical picture of David and little Emily as romantic, fairy-tale child-lovers: "Ah, how I loved her! What happiness (I thought) if we were married, and were going away anywhere to live among the trees and in the fields, never growing older, never growing wiser, children ever . . . in a sweet sleep of purity and peace, and buried by the birds when we were dead!" (10:147). (Dickens's moving into blank verse—as he did in that final pentameter—has been criticized; he told a correspondent that he did it, unconsciously, when he was particularly moved.) But comedy does not exclude more serious anticipatory hints; the description of little Emily as "more of a little woman than I had supposed," following her absorbed interest in David's glowing description of Steerforth, will eventually tell its own tale.

But now the autobiographical fragment takes over, and there can be no doubt of its authenticity of tone ("what I know so well"). Loneliness and neglect are re-experienced with all the agony of a 10-year-old boy (though in fact Dickens was probably 12 when the events he was about to record took place—see Chapter 11): "And now I fell into a state of neglect, which I cannot look back upon without compassion" (10:149). And a page later: "I now approach a period of my life, which I can never lose the remembrance of, while I remember anything; and the recollection of which has often, without my invocation, come before me like a ghost, and haunted happier times" (10:150).

It was a stroke of genius to make the agent for David's employment the Mr. Quinion, of the "Brooks of Sheffield" joke, whom David had met at Lowestoft. There he was purely a worldly, shrewd friend of Murdstone's; now, as the business manager of Murdstone and Grinby's, he is seen and heard as both callous and sinister, utterly appropriate as David's conductor to hell. One sentence gives his tone and its implications. David's employment in the warehouse was Quinion's suggestion, says Murdstone: " 'He having,' Mr. Quinion observed in a low voice, and half turning round, 'no other prospect, Murdstone' " (10:152). The finality of that spells out the end of hope for David.

The mixture of comedy and pathos in the next chapter is the other way round: David's wretchedness as "a little labouring hind in the service of Murdstone and Grinby" begins the chapter; the sheer comic relief of Mr. and Mrs. Micawber ends it. The chapter title, "I begin Life on my own Account, and don't like it", in the deliberate understatement of its irony, hardly masks David's misery; it is not an exaggeration, after the paradise and purgatory of the early chapters, to see David's experience here as the child's vision of hell. Indeed, abandonment of all hope is twice stressed: "The deep remembrance of the sense I had, of being utterly without hope now"; and, more intimately, "I . . . felt my hopes of growing up to be a learned and distinguished man crushed in my bosom" (11:155). The ambience itself is appalling: the decay of the old warehouse, the "squeaking and scuffling of the old grey rats down in the cellars," the dirt and rottenness, all, wrote the mature Dickens, are "of the present instant," all still before him.

But the fear of losing class is just as strong an element in David's suffering. The backgrounds of Mick Walker and Mealy Potatoes, the two boys who work with David, are comically described, but distaste is only too evident, too. Mick Walker's father was, he tells David, a bargeman, who "walked, in a black velvet head-dress, in the Lord

Mayor's Show"; Mealy Potatoes' father was a waterman and had the additional distinction of being a fireman. In addition, "some young relation of Mealy's—I think his little sister—did Imps in the Pantomime" (11:155). David is not the snob that Pip of *Great Expectations* will be; but the next paragraph begins, "No words can express the secret agony of my soul as I sunk into this companionship," and a few pages later, we have this: "I know that I worked from morning until night, with common men and boys, a shabby child" (11:161).

The comic vitality of the Micawbers has an immensely lightening effect after the warehouse agony. An attempt to analyse their power will be made in Chapter 6, but part of it is undoubtedly their parody of gentility, the gentility that David sees threatened by the warehouse experience. A further lightening effect comes from David's own vitality: his ordering of "alamode" beef and the "Genuine Stunning ale" (the subject of one of "Phiz"'s' best illustrations); his dealing with the drunken bookstall-keeper and the would-be educated pawnbroker on Mrs. Micawber's behalf; and his helping Mr. Micawber to prepare his dinner in the King's Bench Prison. Here, too, ending the chapter, is the first—and perhaps the most convincing—claim in the novel that out of such agonies is born the artist: "When I tread the old ground, I do not wonder that I seem to see and pity, going on before me, an innocent romantic boy, making his imaginative world out of such strange experiences and sordid things" (11:169).

The next two chapters, 12 and 13, show that Dickens's "imaginative world" was conjured up just as powerfully as what he had experienced himself. The first part of Chapter 12 is devoted to the Micawbers, to Mrs. Micawber's credo ("I never will desert Mr. Micawber"), rising "into a perfect scream," and to the kiss that she gives David at parting, when they set off for Plymouth ("a mist cleared from her eyes, and she saw what a little creature I really was"), the only sign of love in David's London world before the terrors of his flight to Dover. No such flight ended the young Dickens's experience of the blacking-warehouse; but flights of boys from an unendurable world had haunted his imagination since Oliver Twist's flight to London.

In each incident on the road to Dover a young boy's terrors are vividly re-created. In the first one, involving the long-legged young man with the donkey cart, David is the pursuer, not the pursued; but the breathless immediacy of his pursuit of the thief has much of the agony of Oliver in his flight from the bookstall, hunted down by the "Stop thief!"–shouting mob: "Now I lost him, now I saw him, now I lost him, now I was cut at with a whip, now shouted at, now down in the mud, now up again, now running into somebody's arms, now running headlong at a post" (12:179).

The ending of the number here shows Dickens's great skill in using monthly parts to contribute to maximum suspense. Even before he has started, David has lost everything—and the long Dover Road lies before him.

The two major adventures to follow, when his flight is resumed in the next number, show two of Dickens's gifts at their most powerful: the use of the grotesque and the swift creation of the brutal. In both, the power is greatly increased by their effect on a child's eye and a child's consciousness. The "drunken madman" who eventually buys David's jacket in Chatham is almost literally diabolic. He has, chant the boys who invade his shop, sold himself to the devil, and his extraordinary language—especially the repetition of "goroo!" (invented, of course, by Dickens)—certainly underlines this: " 'Oh, how much for the jacket?' cried the old man, after examining it. 'Oh-goroo!—how much for the jacket?' 'Half-a-crown,' I answered, recovering myself. 'Oh, my lungs and liver,' cried the old man, 'no! Oh, my eyes, no! Oh, my limbs, no! Eighteenpence. Goroo!' " (13:184).

A final grotesque detail shows how much of Dickens's imaginative effect comes from the unexpected, at once made to seem part of the total scene: the old man collapses onto his bed, "yelling in a frantic way, to his own windy tune, the Death of Nelson; with an Oh! before every line, and innumerable Goroos interspersed" (13:185).

The incident of the tinker is brutal by any standards, and immeasurably more so to a sensitive, frightened boy. His knocking down of the woman with him, and threats to do the same or worse to David, are given a realism that shows that powers of both observation and invention are as important to the novel as powers of recollection. But what is just as important at this stage is the stamina, the remarkable perseverance that Dickens gave to the victim of all these adventures;

David's "ultimate pertness . . . almost blitheness," as John Jones puts it so well (135).

That "ultimate pertness" is given its reward in the scene when David finally meets his great-aunt, a scene managed with all of Dickens's theatrical skill: " 'If you please, ma'am,' I began. She started and looked up. 'If you please, aunt.' 'EH?' exclaimed Miss Betsey, in a tone of amazement I have never heard approached. 'If you please, aunt, I am your nephew.' 'Oh, Lord!' said my aunt. And sat flat down in the garden-path" (13:191).

The transition from the hell of the wine warehouse and the flight to Dover to the eccentric haven offered by Betsey Trotwood is done with both confidence and delicacy. It is, above all, a totally new life, for both David and the reader. Betsey Trotwood and Mr. Dick are new people; their eccentricities are not only comic but life-giving, and clearly intended to be so. They have an important role, too, in controlling any temptation to sentimentality offered by an image of peace, obtained at last, however deserved.

David meets—or rather, sees—Mr. Dick first, "a florid, pleasant-looking gentleman, with a grey head, who shut up one eye in a grotesque manner, nodded his head at me several times, shook it at me as often, laughed, and went away" (13:190). This impression is enough to discompose David; but the first draft—which, as John Butt and Kathleen Tillotson first pointed out, Dickens changed in proof—would have added considerably to his fears.[20] There he "put his tongue out against the glass" and "squinted at me in a most terrible manner." The softening of this first description is most important, since Mr. Dick and David are soon to become devoted friends. At the same proof stage, Dickens changed the bull-in-the-china-shop delusion he had given to Mr. Dick to his obsession with King Charles's head; the topical allusion, in the bicentenary year of King Charles I's execution, at least gives the delusion more point. One of Mr. Dick's attractions is that he instinctively understands David; his vast kite is a major bond between them. Betsey Trotwood's treatment of him, as much more intelligent than he looks or his family believes, is, as the novel shows, absolutely right. It reflects the humane treatment of idiots, in which

Dickens intensely believed; but beyond that, she treats Mr. Dick as something of the traditional "Holy Fool" whose inner wisdom often penetrates beyond that of the practical and worldly. Dostoyevski had read *David Copperfield* and confessed his debts to Dickens. We know he admired Mr. Pickwick and the Micawbers; it is tempting to think that his own "Holy Fool," Prince Myshkin in *The Idiot*, may have owed something to Mr. Dick.

Betsey Trotwood herself is a much more complex character: forthright, impetuous, energetic (David particularly notices that she has "a very quick, bright eye"), masculine (she wears a man's gold watch and what seem to be men's shirts), and often comical in her masculine energy, but highly perceptive, deeply affectionate to both Mr. Dick and David—and soon acting as David's fairy godmother. Her attacks on marriage in this chapter hint strongly at the mystery in her past life. Her hatred of trespassing donkeys is the kind of relatively harmless, autocratic eccentricity that goes well with such a woman; Dickens may well have introduced it here to anticipate the marvelous buffeting of the Murdstones and their donkeys in the next chapter. David's reception by his aunt begins comically with the extraordinary mixture of drinks she pours into his mouth as "restoratives"; but the details of her room, which his boy's keen eye observes, "taking note of everything"—"the cat, the kettle-holder, the two canaries, the old china, the punch-bowl full of dried rose-leaves"—quickly establish this as a *home,* David's vital need after the mockery made of his first home by the Murdstones and the horrors of Murdstone and Grinby's. David's memories at the close of the chapter, as he nestles in his white-curtained bed, are made into one of those rests or "spots of time" Dickens loved precisely because they reflect so strongly his own nostalgia for what—particularly during the writing of *David Copperfield*—he felt he had missed: "I remember how I thought of all the solitary places under the night sky where I had slept, and how I prayed that I never might be houseless any more, and never might forget the houseless. I remember how I seemed to float, then, down the melancholy glory of that track upon the sea, away into the world of dreams" (13:199).

Betsey Trotwood's discomfiture of the Murdstones dominates the next chapter, and it is done with all Dickens's skill and enjoyment in enacting a theatrical set piece. The "hurried battle-piece" with the donkeys gives Betsey the advantage from the beginning, and she never loses it. David, fenced into his corner, is, of course, intimately concerned with the contest, and he makes his own contribution to it. But Betsey's pitiless exposure of Murdstone's tyranny and hypocrisy—her constant harping on the disaster of David's mother accepting him as her second husband—goes surely beyond the experience of an 11- or 12-year-old boy. Just as does, we may well feel, the brilliant stroke of realistic irony with which Betsey puts Miss Murdstone into her place early in the interview: "'I consider [says Miss Murdstone] our poor lamented Clara to have been, in all essential respects, a mere child.' 'It is a comfort to you and me, ma'am,' said my aunt, 'who are getting on in life, and are not likely to be made unhappy by our personal attractions, that nobody can say the same of us'" (14:208).

Betsey's strategy from then on, addressing herself only to Mr. Murdstone and ignoring his sister, whose exasperation mounts almost uncontrollably, is, again, totally successful. But its appeal is surely much more an adult reader than to a boy of David's age. Dickens was getting it both ways. He showed David overjoyed at the outcome: his joint adoption by his aunt and Mr. Dick as Trotwood Copperfield, and Mr. Dick hailing "this happy close of the proceedings with repeated bursts of laughter." But at a deliberately higher critical level, he used the whole scene to nail down once and for all the Murdstone characteristics that he so detested: the harshness, cruelty, and hatred masquerading as religion, which had rightly inspired Betsey Trotwood to recall Murdstone's name as "the Murderer."

The chapter does not end the number. But the final paragraph stresses David's emergence from the crisis: "Thus I began my new life, in a new name, and with everything new about me. Now that the state of doubt was over, I felt, for many days, like one in a dream." The paragraph also returns, momentarily, to the most horrendous of the childhood experiences Dickens had entrusted to his autobiographical fragment—returns to give it, as experienced by David, a final closure:

"a curtain had for ever fallen on my life at Murdstone and Grinby's. No one has ever raised that curtain since. I have lifted it for a moment, even in this narrative, with a reluctant hand, and dropped it gladly" (14:215).

The titles of the next two chapters—"I make another Beginning" and "I am a New Boy in more Senses than One"—underline David's new life. As bildungsroman hero, he will be shown making choices, good and bad, that will lead to his ultimate maturity. From now on, the novel is packed with new characters, new plots, new directions; at its center, in David's consciousness, there is a new security. But, inevitably, as we watch the process of David's growing-up, of the disciplining of his romantic heart, the extraordinary intensity of his child's-eye vision—of the compelling way in which Dickens records the joys and agonies of a child—is diminished. Dickens created such a vision only once more, 11 years later, in the early chapters of *Great Expectations*.

Chapter Five

Structure

The chapter entitled "David Copperfield (Month by Month)" in John Butt and Kathleen Tillotson's *Dickens at Work,* giving Dickens's number plans for the novel and the use he made of them, shows the immense care that he took in both planning and writing. A bildungsroman, told in the first person throughout, offers a particular challenge to a master of multiple plots. Everything in the novel must ultimately relate to the hero, if not as part of his own immediate experience then clarifying it by affirmation or criticism or even by simple juxtaposition. David's observation is central to the novel from Chapter 2 ("I Observe") onwards, but it is never detached observation; the host of characters and plots that Dickens created all, in some way, contribute to David's checkered, often painful, but ultimately confident progress to maturity. Several critics have stressed the theme of the undisciplined heart as integral to David's own progress and as the most powerful binder of apparently disparate plots; it obviously plays an important part in the novel's structure.[21] David's love of little Emily in the Yarmouth days is treated as pure, disinterested childish fancy; discipline or indiscipline here seems irrelevant. But his extravagant infatuation for his schoolboy loves—Miss Shepherd and the eldest Miss Larkins—ironically treated as it is, shows where his danger lies. It also shows that he is his mother's son. Clara Copperfield is presented as charming, spontaneous, loving, although "pettish" and "wilful" as well; even the child David quickly recognizes her weakness. "I knew as well, when I saw my mother's head lean down upon [Murdstone's] shoulder, and her arm touch his neck—I knew as well that he could mould her pliant nature into any form he chose, as I know, now, that he did it" (4:45). Clara's romantic, undisciplined heart leads to her disastrous marriage to Murdstone, and it is surely not driving Dickens's love of interconnectedness too far to see the major tragedy of the novel, Steerforth's seduction of Emily, as owing something at least to David's equally romantic hero worship of his Byronic friend. It is not only that David introduces Steerforth to the Peggotty family, however unconscious he is of the consequences, but that he presents Steerforth as totally godlike ("such a generous, fine, noble fellow"). Dickens went to great pains to show the reader Steerforth's feet as clay. The opening paragraph of Chapter 32, following immediately the misery caused by Emily's flight with Steerforth, is a brilliant piece of psychological analysis into David's feelings. "What is natural in me, is natural in many other men, I infer, and so I am not afraid to write that I had never loved Steerforth better than when the ties that bound me to him were broken" (32:455).

That shows the strength and loyalty of a young man's hero worship; but it also shows the power and irrationality of what, later in the novel, Dickens was to call the "mistaken impulse of an undisciplined heart." This is the phrase used by Annie Strong in Chapter 45 when, kneeling at her husband's feet, she confesses her childish love for her cousin Jack Maldon before her marriage to Dr. Strong and before her knowledge of her cousin's "false and thankless heart." Before this climax, the Dr. Strong and Annie subplot may have seemed disconnected with David's story. In his number plan for this chapter Dickens showed clearly how close he intended the connection to be: "'No disparity in marriage like unsuitability of mind and purpose'— 'Saved from the first mistaken impulse of an undisciplined heart'—

'My love was founded on a rock—': all brought to bear on David, and applied by him to himself." These phrases are all Annie's; they are all repeated at the end of the chapter, as they go through David's mind. We have seen David's heart as undisciplined in his uncritical acceptance of Steerforth. It is apparently even more so in both his marriage to Dora and his blindness to Agnes's love for him. Dickens clearly intended this contrast as central. "Introduction of the real heroine" is his memorandum note when David first meets Agnes in Canterbury, and this number, following the crisis of Betsey Trotwood's financial ruin, contrasts the "rock" of Agnes's love with the absurdly impractical charm of Dora's in the strongest way possible. It is Agnes who finds David the post of secretary to Dr. Strong, in Chapter 35, and Dora who, in Chapter 37 ("A little Cold Water"), responds to his earnest plans to work and earn their "crust": "Oh, yes; but I don't want to hear any more about crusts! . . . And Jip must have a mutton-chop every day at twelve, or he'll die!" (540). And at the end of the chapter: "'Now, don't get up at five o'clock, you naughty boy. It's so nonsensical!' 'My love,' said I, 'I have work to do.' 'But don't do it!' returned Dora. 'Why should you?' (37:544).

"Silly" and "light-headed," indeed, and we hardly need Betsey's probings to see this. With Agnes's love in mind, utterly unrecognized as it is by David, Betsey's comment on David seems justified enough: "Blind, blind, blind!" Without knowing why, as she repeats it, David feels "a vague unhappy loss or want of something overshadow [him] like a cloud" (35:504). Dickens pressed the point home at the end of the chapter, with obvious verbal irony: thinking of Agnes's "calm seraphic eyes," David hears a beggar muttering, "as if he were an echo of the morning: 'Blind! Blind! Blind!'" (35:519).

But does Dickens *over*press the point? Dora may, like David's mother (and the parallel is important), be willful, pettish, and light-headed; she may totally abjure the doctrine of work, which Dickens himself believed in so fervently; but she has all the sexual charm and provocativeness that Agnes so conspicuously lacks (This contrast between the two will be discussed in Chapter 7). But it is Dora's charm that provides a subtext for the affectionately ironical chapters that treat of their short married life. In his number plan for Chapter 44 ("Our Housekeeping"), Dickens wrote, "Carry through incapacity of Dora—but affectionate," and this mixture, of incapacity and affection, is dominant to the end. Dora may be exasperating as a housekeeper, but it is impossible not to share David's love for her. The details are comically memorable: the salmon that she walked miles and miles for and that cost "one pound six"; the little dinner for Traddles, with the oysters unopened and Jip occupying the center of the table (marvelously illustrated by "Phiz"); the succession of appalling servants; Dora's anxious desire to hold David's pens while he writes.

Both texts meet in Chapter 48 ("Domestic"), the most serious and inward examination of their marriage. Dora's instinctive love and emotional wisdom, her realization that, whatever David's plans to change her, she must remain herself, are presented with all Dickens's delicacy of touch: "'It's better for me to be stupid than uncomfortable, isn't it?' said Dora. 'Better to be naturally Dora than anything else in the world.' 'In the world! Ah, Doady, it's a large place!'" (48:696). David's attempts to "form her mind" ("I read Shakespeare to her—and fatigued her to the last degree") are presented with the irony they deserve.

But set against that is David's unhappiness. It forms a strong, honestly faced strand of this chapter: "The old unhappy feeling pervaded my life. It was deepened, if it were changed at all; but it was as undefined as ever, and addressed me like a strain of sorrowful music faintly heard in the night. I loved my wife dearly, and I was happy; but the happiness I had vaguely anticipated once, was not the happiness I enjoyed, and there was always something wanting" (48:697).

Dickens makes it only too clear from where this unhappiness stems: "'The first mistaken impulse of an undisciplined heart.' These words of Mrs. Strong's were constantly recurring to me, at this time; were almost always present to my mind. . . . 'There can be no disparity in marriage, like unsuitability of mind and purpose.' Those words I remembered too" (48:698).

In the short chapter devoted to Dora's death (Chapter 53, "Another Retrospect"), the phrase is repeated twice more: "As I look out on the night, my tears fall fast, and my undisciplined heart is chastened—heavily." And a few moments later, repeating what Dora had said a page before, "Would it, indeed, have been better if we had loved each other as a boy and girl, and forgotten it? Undisciplined heart, reply!" (768).

There can be no doubt that this theme is central to the structure of the novel. It links David's mother and her disastrous remarriage; Annie Strong's sufferings from her early infatuation for the ignoble Jack Maldon; Betsey Trotwood's fears from her mysterious, worthless husband; above all, David's uncritical worship of Steerforth, which leads to Emily's seduction and the end of the Peggottys' happiness; and his immature love for the light-headed Dora, which leads to his feeling that "there was always something wanting."

But a bildungsroman can cherish immaturity, too; countering the criticism of the "undisciplined heart," Dickens was honest—or realistic—enough to show us both Steerforth's inborn powers of attraction, the "spell" he wields, and Dora's palpable charms. With Dora, indeed, he was drawing on his own early unsuccessful love affair with Maria Beadnell. Five years after *David Copperfield*, when she was Mrs. Winter and they were in touch again, he wrote to her (on 15 February 1855): "I fancy . . . that you may have seen in one of my books a faithful reflection of the passion I had for you, and may have thought that it was something to have been loved so well, and may have seen in little bits of 'Dora' touches of your own self sometimes and a grace here and there that may be revived in your little girls, years hence, for the bewilderment of some other young lover—though he will never be as terribly in earnest as I and David Copperfield were" (*Letters* [Nonesuch]:2:629).

But whatever the delights and sorrows of the subtext, the "real heroine," as Dickens called her, is Agnes, and the novel's structure demands—with all David's blindness to her love, maintained until two chapters before the end—that the reader at least should know that they will ultimately marry. Dickens twice reminded himself in his memoranda notes of the importance of this central theme: "Carry the thread of Agnes through it all" (for no. XII, Chapters 35–37), and

"Agnes. Carry through" (for no. XVIII, Chapters 54–57). Dora herself helps to carry the thread. After the disasters of her first dinner party for Traddles, she says, "I wish that I could have gone down into the country for a whole year, and lived with Agnes! . . . I think she might have improved me, and I think I might have learned from *her*" (44:643). It is Agnes whom Dora calls to her deathbed (for what she says to Agnes we have to wait until the end of Chapter 62), and Agnes who breaks the news to David (whatever we may think of Dickens's rhetoric here): "—That face, so full of pity, and of grief, that rain of tears, that awful mute appeal to me, that solemn hand upraised toward Heaven!" (53:768). Agnes is intimately linked to Uriah Heep's machinations against her father, the more so because of his sexual designs on her; she is present at Micawber's great unmasking of Heep and at its aftermath. It is Agnes's letter that lifts the cloud of David's despondency in Switzerland and encourages him to continue his writing; and finally, two of the last four chapters (Chapter 60, entitled "Agnes," and Chapter 62, "A Light shines on my Way"—with "Agnes—" added on the number plan) lead up to David's declaration of love and their marriage. The fact that the reader certainly anticipates her first response, "I have loved you all my life!" and may well have anticipated her second, and that Dora, on her deathbed, leaves her a last charge, "That only I would occupy this vacant place" (both phrases are in the number plan), shows how successfully Dickens had fulfilled his design and carried "the thread of Agnes through it all."

To underline the irrevocableness of the other main plot of the novel, Steerforth's seduction of little Emily, Dickens used a number of structural devices: omens, emblems, deliberate anticipations, a skillful use of the sinister, all of which evoke a sense of fate. They begin early, with the long interpolation Dickens made in proof to the scene of David and little Emily as children at Yarmouth, and Emily's confession that she would like to be "a lady," followed by her running out to sea and David's comment (see 3:34–36). They continue with the gossip among the other girls at Omer & Joram's in Chapter 21, again, on the same theme of Emily's wanting to be a lady. And by now it is clear that Steerforth will be her seducer. This gives his conversation with

Rosa Dartle, just before he sets off with David to see the Peggottys, a sharply ironical, anticipatory force. Rosa says, "'That sort of people. Are they really animals and clods, and beings of another order? I want to know *so* much.' 'Why, there's a pretty wide separation between them and us,' said Steerforth, with indifference. 'They are not to be expected to be as sensitive as we are. Their delicacy is not to be shocked, or hurt very easily'" (20:294).

The next chapter, describing David and Steerforth together in Yarmouth, undermines Steerforth further and points strongly toward the seduction. The phrases that Dickens put into David's analysis of how Steerforth's effortless superiority *might* be seen point unerringly to Steerforth's real character: "a brilliant game, played . . . in a mere wasteful careless course of winning what was worthless to him, and next moment thrown away." Steerforth's own comment on Ham, as they leave after the celebration of Ham's engagement to little Emily, shocks even David: "That's rather a chuckle-headed fellow for the girl; isn't he?" A final comment ends the chapter: "Daisy, I believe you are in earnest, and are good. I wish we all were!" (21:317–18). It is as clear as Dickens wished to make it that Steerforth will seduce little Emily and plunge his hosts into misery. But the following chapter both turns the screw more tightly and adds another dimension. It first continues Steerforth's note of remorseful anticipation: "David, I wish to God I had had a judicious father these last twenty years! . . . I wish with all my soul I had been better guided. . . . I wish with all my soul I could guide myself better!" (22:322). Then Dickens conjures up fate in one of his favorite ways—here, by Steerforth's twice quoting *Macbeth:* "Why, being gone, I am a man again"; followed at once by, "And now for dinner! If I have not (Macbeth-like) broken up the feast with most admired disorder, Daisy" (22:323). Two further remarks of Steerforth's, some chapters later, when he arrives at David's after his dinner party for Traddles and the Micawbers, condemn his ruthlessness from his own mouth: "Don't you remember Traddles? Traddles in our room at Salem House?" asks David. "'Oh! That fellow!' said Steerforth, beating a lump of coal on the top of the fire, with the poker. 'Is he as soft as ever?'" As David notes, he continues "idly beating on the lump of coal with the poker" (28:424–25). His second remark a few minutes later, on the news that Barkis is dying, is more disturbing in its implications: "'No! Ride on! Rough-shod if need be, smooth-shod if that will do, but ride on! Ride on over all obstacles, and win the race!' 'And win what race?' said I. 'The race that one has started in,' said he. 'Ride on!'" (28:426).

Three further characters played their different parts in the early chapters in suggesting the irrevocableness of little Emily's fate. The first, Martha Endell, a prostitute ("The girl already lost" in the number plan), is at this point only an emblem, though she will play an important part in the plot later. But as an emblem of little Emily's possible fate, dogging her heels as she walks behind Emily and Ham across the Yarmouth sands, she is powerfully presented; it is Steerforth who is immediately arrested by her sudden appearance: "'That is a black shadow to be following the girl,' said Steerforth, standing still; 'what does it mean?' He spoke in a low voice that sounded almost strange to me. 'She must have it in her mind to beg of them, I think,' said I. 'A beggar would be no novelty,' said Steerforth; 'but it is a strange thing that the beggar should take that shape to-night.' 'Why?' I asked him. 'For no better reason, truly, than because I was thinking,' he said, after a pause, 'of something like it, when it came by'" (22:326). That is fine, compressed writing; if it foreshadows what could well be little Emily's fate, it also penetrates Steerforth's dark and, here, at least, guilty conscience.

The other two characters, Steerforth's servant Littimer and the dwarf Miss Mowcher, are both clearly intended to play important roles as Steerforth's evil instruments. Littimer plays his to perfection; Miss Mowcher, after one marvelously comic and sinister scene, had to be amended by Dickens after her model, Mrs. Seymour Hill, a manicurist, threatened legal proceedings.

Littimer is a brilliant study in hypocrisy: "He surrounded himself with an atmosphere of respectability, and walked secure in it. It would have been next to impossible to suspect him of anything wrong, he was so thoroughly respectable" (22:299). The later description of little Emily's elopement shows the important part he plays in it.

Miss Mowcher, in her one major scene, is one of the most over-powering and blackly comic voices in the novel and will be discussed in that role (see Chapter 6). But behind the exuberance and the boasted volatility there is a strong sense of sexual corruption and a clear willingness to abet Steerforth in his designs. Indeed, having forced Emily's name out of them, she is as explicit as she dare be in front of David: "Ah! what's that game at forfeits? I love my love with an E, because she's enticing; I hate her with an E, because she's en-gaged. I took her to the sign of the exquisite, and treated her with an elopement; her name's Emily, and she lives in the east? Ha! ha! ha! Mr. Copperfield, ain't I volatile?" (22:334).

The dignity and pathos of the letter Mrs. Hill instructed her sol-icitor to write to Dickens, requesting him to change the character, show how justified she was. The change of heart Dickens gave Miss Mowcher in Chapter 32 when she calls on David ("Take a word of advice, even from three foot nothing. Try not to associate bodily de-fects with mental, my good friend, except for a solid reason" [464]) is as skillfully done as it could be, as is her later capture of the disguised Littimer and her being "highly complimented by the Bench" at his trial and "cheered right home to her lodgings." But the comic and corrupt Miss Mowcher is a splendid part of the novel, and Dickens never did anyone quite like her again.

The deaths of both Steerforth and Ham in the great storm are carefully prepared. Almost immediately after Emily's elopement, Ham, on the beach at Yarmouth, is made to point "confusedly out to sea"—and we are left in little doubt as to what his eventual fate will be: "Ay, Mas'r Davy. I don't rightly know how 'tis, but from over yon there seemed to me to come—the end of it like" (32:457).

One detail of Steerforth's drowned body, etched in at the end of the storm chapter—"I saw him lying with his head upon his arm, as I had often seen him lie at school"—is several times anticipated; most vividly when David sees him for the last time at Highgate: "But he slept—let me think of him so again—as I had often seen him sleep at school; and thus, in this silent hour, I left him" (29:437).

This one physical detail has almost the force of a musical leitmotiv, and it appears in both the chapter summary and among the memoranda, there prefaced "To remember" (twice underlined).

David himself is given a premonition of the storm long before it happens, in one of those "spots of time" ending with a time switch between the young man experiencing and the older man writing that is central to the novel's structure. As he leaves Mrs. Steerforth and Rosa Dartle in their Highgate home at twilight: "Here and there, some early lamps were seen to twinkle in the distant city; and in the eastern quarter of the sky the lurid light still hovered. But, from the greater part of the broad valley interposed, a mist was rising like a sea, which, mingling with the darkness, made it seem as if the gathering waters would encompass them. I have reason to remember this, and think of it with awe; for before I looked upon those two again, a stormy sea had risen to their feet" (46:673–74).

The storm scene itself (Chapter 55, "Tempest") is written not only with great power but with a remarkable sense of immediacy: "As plainly as I behold what happened, I will try to write it down. I do not recall it, but see it done; for it happens again before me" (784). Broadstairs, where he was writing the chapter, contributed, for the chapter summary includes the detail: *"flakes of foam seen at Broadstairs here, last night.* Flying in blotches." It was the climax of Dickens's public reading of the novel and, not surprisingly, his favorite incident. The sounds are as frightening as the visual details: the firing of signal guns, the falling of houses in the town, the thunder of cannon David hears in his sleep, and, above all, the bell ringing on the sinking ship. Ham, plunging into the sea to the rescue, and Steerforth, obviously by now the lone surviving figure, clinging to the mast and waving his "singular red cap" to the watchers on the shore, are brought closer and closer together, until, with a final stroke of irony, their bodies are washed up, one after the other, on the same beach, Steerforth's "among the ruins of the home he had wronged" (44:795). To Forster Dickens wrote on 15 September 1850: "I have been tremendously at work these two days; eight hours at a stretch yesterday, and six hours and a half to-day, with the Ham and Steerforth chapter, which has completely knocked me over—utterly defeated me!"

(*Letters* 6:169). And to two other friends he described himself, during the next two days, as in a "paroxysm of Copperfield"; in the second letter, to W. H. Wills, subeditor of *Household Words*, he claimed to be "having my most powerful effect in all the Story, on the Anvil."

Dickens has often been criticized for the number of coincidences in his novels, but they serve (some better than others, of course) one of his most profoundly held beliefs: in the connectedness of the apparently unconnected. This would be the major, highly serious theme of his next novel, *Bleak House*, as he made quite clear: "What connexion can there have been between many people in the innumerable histories of this world, who, from opposite sides of great gulfs, have, nevertheless, been very curiously brought together!" (*Bleak House*, Chapter 16). The coincidences in *Copperfield*, particularly unexpected meetings—and there are plenty of them—hardly establish interconnection as the main theme, but they play a vital part in the novel's structure.

David's unexpected meeting of Steerforth in the Golden Cross Inn, after they have both been, separately, to Covent Garden, leads quite naturally to David's taking him to visit the Peggottys and so ultimately to his seduction of little Emily. But it is helped by two further coincidences: little Emily's desire to be a lady and Steerforth's unexpectedly meeting—and, of course, charming—Mr. Peggotty and Ham when they visit David at Salem House. The final coincidence in the storm scene, that Steerforth should be a passenger on the Portuguese schooner and Ham the fearless leader of the Yarmouth fishermen, can claim the same kind of irrevocableness as Dickens established in *Bleak House*.

The reappearances of the Murdstones seem to be stretching coincidence very far; but it is important that the early destructive part they play in tyrannizing over both David and his mother should not be forgotten. And they are all in character: Miss Murdstone, as companion to Dora, stealing and exposing David's love letter to her; Mr. Murdstone applying for a license to marry a girl just of age, with beauty and money; and, above all, the annihilating observations on them by Mrs. Chillip, in Chapter 59, relayed to David by her husband,

the doctor who brought him into the world. We also have more ex-
plicitly confirmed the perversity of the Murdstone "religion." "Mrs.
Chillip," says her husband, "quite electrified me, by pointing out that
Mr. Murdstone sets up an image of himself, and calls it the Divine
Nature." "And do you know I must say, sir," he ends, "that I don't
find authority for Mr. and Miss Murdstone in the New Testament?"
"I never found it either!" says David/Dickens (59:833–34).

The Micawber reappearances are on quite a different footing:
comic characters have the right to transcend time and place and rational expectation. But it is also important to the buoyancy of the
whole novel that we should never lose sight of them for long. Micawber's recognition of David through the open door of the Heeps' house
and walking in to claim him—"Copperfield! Is it possible?"—has,
then, its own comic justification; but this does not prevent Micawber
from attempting to give it a philosophical explanation too: "This is
indeed a meeting which is calculated to impress the mind with a sense
of the instability and uncertainty of all human—in short, it is a most
extraordinary meeting." (17:256). We are at once on familiar Micawber territory.

That, ten chapters later, Traddles should be lodging with the Micawbers—just as David had as a boy—seems almost in the nature of
things. It allows another meeting between Micawber and David ("Is
it possible! Have I the pleasure of again beholding Copperfield!"), and
it leads to the shockingly cooked dinner party (one of three such comic
set pieces in the novel) given by David to Traddles and the Micawbers.
But the final Micawber coincidence—that his "gauntlet" flung to the
world as an advertisement for employment should be answered by
Heep (extremely unlikely as it may seem in the everyday world)—is
vital to the climax of one of the major subplots of the novel: Micawber's exposure, deftly assisted by Traddles, of Heep's criminal machinations against Mr. Wickfield.

One of the final (and most far-fetched) coincidences in the novel
is the reappearance of Uriah Heep and Littimer in the model prison,
of which Creakle of Salem House, now a Middlesex magistrate, is
one of the governors (Chapter 61, "I am shown two Interesting

Penitents"). The satire follows closely Dickens's attack on solitary con-
finement and the overfeeding of prisoners at Pentonville in an article
in *Household Words,* "Pet Prisoners," six months before (27 April
1850). Several reviewers at the time noted the closeness of this to Carlyle's essay, "Model Prisons."[22] But far-fetched as the chapter is—and
rare as such social satire is in the novel—it was a brilliant stroke to
show the hypocrisy we have already seen as the ruling passion of both
Heep and Littimer now established as part of "a system," just as it was
to make the coarse, brutal Creakle totally taken in by it. The presen-
tation of Uriah Heep "reading a Hymn Book" and of Littimer, also
"reading a good book," and the homilies they deliver to the assembled
magistrates and visitors are in Dickens's best satirical manner. The
scene, as they each confess their past "follies," mixed with as much
malice as they can muster against David, is pure theater. The "Phiz"
illustration visualizes them perfectly: Heep and Littimer at their most
sanctimonious, as they read their good books; the visitors totally naive
and delighted; the two warders grinning knowingly. It is one of the
warders who supplies the facts behind the façade, when David asks
what the two prisoners' last "follies" were: Number Twenty Seven's
(Uriah Heep's), replies the warder, was "fraud, forgery, and conspir-
acy. . . . Sentence, transportation for life"; Twenty Eight (Littimer),
also transportation, robbed his young master of £250 (61:855).

The final word is, of course, Dickens's, harsher than any tone we
recognize as David's: "It would have been in vain to represent to such
a man as the worshipful Mr. Creakle, that Twenty Seven and Twenty
Eight were perfectly consistent and unchanged; that exactly what they
were then, they had always been; that the hypocritical knaves were
just the subjects to make that sort of profession in such a place . . . in
a word, that it was a rotten, hollow, painfully suggestive piece of business altogether" (61:856).

In the penultimate chapter of the novel (Chapter 63, "A Visitor"),
Mr. Peggotty visits from Australia; without this visit, David says "one
thread in the web I have spun would have a ravelled end." But, again,
this is the Dickens voice: proud of the "web" he has "spun," proud,
too, that—as in all his novels—there will be no "ravelled end" but a

roundup of all the characters, major and minor. In his last novel, *Dombey and Son*, he had Florence's dog, Diogenes, added in proof; here, he took two chapters to make sure that every character of note makes a reappearance, if only by mention.

Mr. Peggotty's news is, naturally, the most important, and it does much to establish the glow of confidence that generations of readers have found so appealing in the end of the novel. Little Emily is, as we should expect, as restored as she can be, helping both her uncle and other settlers; Martha is married to a settler (the hope offered to re-formed prostitutes in Angela Burdett-Coutts's Home for Homeless Women). Mrs. Gummidge is so recovered from thinking of the "old' un" that, in a marvelous last touch of comedy, she can respond to a ship's cook's proposal of marriage by laying a bucket over his head, "till he sung out fur help, and I went in and reskied of him," says Mr. Peggotty. Mr. Peggotty himself is a prosperous farmer.

But the major revelation is that Mr. Micawber is now a magistrate, his thriving family settled in Port Middlebay, and Mr. Mell, now Doctor Mell, is headmaster of "Colonial Salem-House Grammar School." Realistically, this is, of course, all much too far-fetched to be plausible; but this is a fairy-tale ending, a wish fulfillment that reflects a more poetic justice than the everyday world allows. And even realistically, we may well feel that Micawber must still be an infinitely better magistrate than Creakle. That Mell should name his school after Salem House, where he had suffered so wretchedly, is either an instance of Dickens's over-tidying up or a joke that hardly comes off. But in the report of the public dinner for Micawber—clearly written by Micawber himself—and in Micawber's letter to David, in the same newspaper, congratulating him on his "soaring flight" as a writer, Dickens did not put a foot wrong.

The final short chapter, "A Last Retrospect" (the last of four such "retrospects"), has a mellowness of its own. Shortly before finishing it, on 21 October 1850, Dickens told Forster that he was "within three pages of the shore"; the sense of reaching a goal, of coming home, is all-important. The chapter begins and ends with Agnes, symbol of David's own home, long now recognized as the rock it is, as we would expect it to be. But as David conjures up, one by one, the three characters who have most loved and protected him—Betsey Trotwood, Peggotty, and Mr. Dick—he summons up at the same time the homes *they* had given him and the objects that symbolized them: the "bit of wax candle, a yard measure in a little house, and a work-box with a picture of St. Paul's upon the lid"; the "Crocodile-Book," now kept by Peggotty as "a precious relic"; and Mr. Dick's giant kites. The last home he summons up is that of the lovable Traddles, now happily married to Sophy, with the best bedrooms reserved for "the Beauty and the girls."

But in between is what was once the Steerforth home, conjured up in its misery by one horrifying vignette: "Looking fixedly at me, [Mrs. Steerforth] puts her hand to her forehead, and moans. Suddenly she cries, in a terrible voice, 'Rosa, come to me. He is dead!' Rosa kneeling at her feet, by turns caresses her, and quarrels with her; now fiercely telling her, 'I loved him better than you ever did!'—now soothing her to sleep on her breast, like a sick child. Thus I leave them; thus I always find them; thus they wear their time away, from year to year" (64:875).

Two more vignettes complete the faces David calls up so vividly: first, the grotesque picture of Dora's friend, Julia Mills, now "married to a growling old Scotch Croesus with great flaps of ears" and "steeped in money to the throat," the symbol of her own phrase, when things were going wrong between David and Dora, "the Desert of Sahara"; and as part of that desert, which Julia calls "society," Jack Maldon, still sneering at Dr. Strong, his benefactor. And secondly, Dr. Strong himself, still laboring at his dictionary and "happy in his home and wife."

This roundup of characters, preceded by Mrs. Chillip's biting observations on the Murdstones and the exposure of Uriah Heep and Littimer, is, then, anything but arbitrary; it is part of a structure that draws a clear line between the true and the false, openness and hypocrisy, generous love and cold-hearted indifference.

One other, more formal structural device remains to be examined. Dickens believed intensely in life's mixture, in what Shakespeare, drawing on Montaigne, had called, in *All's Well That Ends Well*, "The web of our life . . . of a mingled yarn, good and ill together." *David Copperfield* has that "mingled yarn" in abundance, and to show it, Dickens used one device in particular: a deliberate switching of tones within chapters or monthly numbers. Most (but not all) of the monthly numbers contain three chapters; the twenty numbers of *Copperfield* (the last two a double number, as usual) contain 64. The first four numbers, Chapters 1–12, devoted to David's own immediate experience, give abundant examples of switching of tones within chapters and monthly numbers. They also show how skillfully Dickens used the monthly part division to raise curiosity and suspense, often by anticipation, at the end of many numbers—an essential skill to keep his first vast readership always interested.

Chapter 1 does more than record David's birth; it introduces the character who will, in many ways, dominate the last two-thirds of the novel. It is clear that Betsey Trotwood will at some point return, with an important role to play (Dickens would never waste such an eccentric, full-blooded character); but at this point Dickens gave nothing away. The next two chapters, completing the first number, are mainly happy: David in his home, with his mother and Peggotty, and then in his second home, the boat at Yarmouth. But in each chapter menace is skillfully suggested: in Chapter 2 by the "Brooks of Sheffield" joke between Murdstone and Quinion, bewildering to the young David; and at the end of Chapter 3—more frightening because of its sharp juxtaposition with the paradise of the Peggotty boat—menace appears in the sheer presence of Murdstone as David's new stepfather.

Chapter 4, which begins the next number, fully justifies that sense of menace. Despite the saving grace of David's mother and Peggotty, its tone, for David, is almost uniformly wretched: the Murdstones, drawing in for the kill, the caning, the biting, David's imprisonment in his room. But there is one important and moving juxtaposition between the final event of the chapter and the opening one of the next. At the end of Chapter 4 Miss Murdstone, at her coldest, takes leave of David as he goes off to school and says on the way that "she hoped I would repent, before I came to a bad end." Chapter 5 opens with

Peggotty wordlessly squeezing David "to her stays" (the detail says a lot) and giving him cakes and a purse of money. That sets the tone for a chapter that is relatively cheerful, after the last one, until the affliction of David's placard: "Take care of him. He bites." And despite his dread as to how the boys will respond, Mr. Mell's obvious fondness for him keeps this happier tone going to the chapter's end.

Chapter 6, the last one of the number, is cheerful, too, dominated by Steerforth and his protection of David. His disposal of David's money anticipates much in his character; but the striking end of the chapter anticipates much more. Steerforth's apparently innocuous inquiry as to whether David has a sister suggests already someone with a cavalier attitude to women: "That's a pity," says Steerforth, when he learns that David hasn't. "If you had had one, I should think she would have been a pretty, timid, little, bright-eyed sort of girl. I should have liked to know her" (6:87). The final vignette, as David looks at him in bed, "with his handsome face turned up, and his head reclining easily on his arm," is the first of the deliberate warnings of his death (as we know much later in the novel). But what follows conjures up menace in the very act of denying it: "No veiled future dimly glanced upon him in the moonbeams. There was no shadowy picture of his footsteps, in the garden that I dreamed of walking in all night" (6:88).

The next chapter, "My 'First Half' at Salem House," has a great range of tones: contempt for Creakle's ignorant brutality, pity for Mr. Mell's ill usage, David's enjoyment at reading his books aloud to Steerforth, his pleasure at Mr. Peggotty's and Ham's visit, his pride in Steerforth. David's feelings of happiness come to a climax in the chapter that follows, "My Holidays. Especially one Happy Afternoon." But from then on, everything goes downhill: David "as sulky as a bear!" (Miss Murdstone's observation); obeying "like a dog" (his own); eating his meals in silence and embarrassment. We are not prepared for the shock of his mother's death, which opens Chapter 9, the last of the number, but Dickens has made quite clear what its effect on the Murdstones' treatment of David will be. Before that we have the bold—and Shakespearean—mixture of tones that preface the funeral itself: the cheerfulness of Mr. Omer and the lovemaking of Minnie and Joram, interspersed, as they reach Blunderstone, with David's tears.

The last of these early numbers (Chapters 10–12) will take us to the nadir of David's fortunes. But to make the contrast sharper, Dickens gives us in Chapter 10 a cheerful, innocent interval before the descent: David's return to the Peggottys, Peggotty's marriage to Barkis, the last, happy manifestations of David's boyhood love for little Emily. But the chapter ends on a very different note: David's state of neglect, followed by the sinister introduction by Murdstone of Murdstone and Grinby's warehouse: "Mr. Quinion suggests that it gives employment to some other boys, and that he sees no reason why it shouldn't, on the same terms, give employment to you" (10:152). The agony of Murdstone and Grinby's is tellingly mixed with the comedy of the Micawbers; the mixture keeps the pervasive—and justified—self-pity of the chapter under control. Just as, in the next chapter, when David begins his flight to Dover, the long-legged young man with the donkey cart begins a series of grotesque incidents that add their own tone to David's desperation.

Chapter Six

Voices

David *Copperfield* has its full quota of comic and near-comic characters; most of them, as in all Dickens's novels, are instantly recognizable by their voices. Both the Micawbers have phrases that have passed into the language: "Something will turn up," "I never will desert Mr. Micawber." And they have, of course, the great additional interest of being inspired, to some extent at least, by Dickens's own mother and father, Elizabeth and John Dickens. The parallels between the Micawbers' precarious state in London, when the young David boards with them, and the Dickens family's similar state when the young Dickens worked in Warren's blacking-warehouse, are obvious. And a glance at one of John Dickens's begging letters shows the clear source of Micawber's grandiloquence. This was written from Devonshire to Coutts & Company, Dickens's bankers, in March 1842, a few months before John and Elizabeth returned to London: his "preparatory demonstrations of migration," he said, had led to "what may be considered a vote of 'want of confidence,'" which tended "very much to the embarrassment of [his] financial arrangements," and he asked for £25.[23] Forster indeed credits him with one remark that it is hard to believe Micawber did *not* make to his wife about her family: "The Supreme Being must be an entirely different individual from what I have every reason to believe Him to be, if He would care in the least for the society of your relations" (Forster, 552).

The relationship between Mrs. Micawber and Elizabeth Dickens is more complex, but the bitterness that had made Mrs. Nickleby, an admitted portrait of his mother, vain and ridiculous, has gone; Mrs. Micawber may be comically impractical, but the voice we remember is that of an unswervingly loyal wife. And we should never forget that the Micawbers were not in fact David's real parents or responsible for his suffering; hence they could be laughed at without resentment.[24]

Micawber is a comic giant, a Falstaffian figure; Mrs. Micawber, at her most eloquent, is entirely fit to be his wife. Both give, with Sam Weller, Pecksniff, and Sairey Gamp, the most vivid verbal performances in Dickens; all of them, as V. S. Pritchett has said, "do not talk to one another; they talk to themselves."[25]

And there can be no doubt of Dickens's own fondness for both his creations. During the writing of *Copperfield*, he could not resist quoting from them in his letters. "I write," he said to John Leech, "as my friend Mr. Micawber says, 'with a sickly mask of mirth'"; (*Letters* 5:620) "I suppose (like Mr. Micawber), that Something will turn up," he wrote to W. H. Wills (*Letters* 6:157); and to Forster, on the day before his own Dora was born: "Mrs. Micawber is still, I regret to say, in *statu quo*. Ever yours, —WILKINS MICAWBER" (*Letters* 6:148). On the day of the birth itself, he turned to Mrs. Micawber: "What Mrs. Micawber calls 'the unconscious stranger' has so put me out." (*Letters* 6:151). Seven years later, in September 1857, Micawber was still there to give him the phrase—and the analogue—he needed: "If I were not like Mr. Micawber, 'falling back for a spring' on Monday, I think I should slink into a corner and cry" (*Letters* [Nonesuch]:2:875).

Other characters are given one catchphrase that ensures them a comic place in the novel, much more than voices though they are: "Barkis is willing," and Mr. Dick's "King Charles's head." "Donkeys, Janet!" is much too much a part of Betsey Trotwood's psychic makeup to be dismissible as a catchphrase, but she would be a poorer character without it. As would Mrs. Gummidge without her constant lament (so liked by Carlyle), "I am a lone lorn creetur, and everythink goes contrairy with me." But Dickens's psychology was unerring; once the crisis comes and Mr. Peggotty takes little Emily to Australia, Mrs. Gummidge entirely fulfills her promises: "I know you think that I am lone and lorn; but, deary love, 'tan't so no more! I ain't sat here, so long, a-watching, and a-thinking of your trials, without some good being done me" (51:740). As David had commented before, on her impressive change: "I could not meditate enough upon the lesson that I read in Mrs. Gummidge, and the new experience she unfolded to me" (32:459). Creakle is both more and less than a comic character: a tyrant, but a buffoon. He has, literally, no voice, but his whisper, echoed as a roar by his henchman Tungay, is a grotesque part of the spirit of Salem House.

Even relatively minor characters are given consistent roles that they will perform whenever chance permits: Mr. Spenlow, Dora's father, will produce his partner in Doctors' Commons, the "immovable" Jorkins (in fact, "a mild man of a heavy temperament"), whenever he is asked a concession: "No. I will not say what consideration I might give to that point myself, Mr. Copperfield, if I were unfettered. Mr. Jorkins is immovable." Dora's bosom friend Julia Mills, "being understood to have retired from the world on her awful stock of experience," has her portentous rhetoric at hand to meet any crisis. A tiff of jealousy between David and Dora is meat and drink to her: "Enough of this," says Miss Mills, "with an almost venerable air." "Do not allow a trivial misunderstanding to wither the blossoms of spring, which, once put forth and blighted, cannot be renewed. I speak," says Miss Mills, "from experience of the past—the remote irrevocable past. The gushing fountains which sparkle in the sun must not be stopped in mere caprice; the oasis in the desert of Sahara must not be plucked up idly" (33:484–85). It is hardly surprising that Julia and the journal relating to Dora she keeps after the crisis of Spenlow's death are David's only consolation: "Wednesday. D. comparatively cheerful. Sang to her, as congenial melody, Evening Bells. Effect not soothing, but reverse, D. inexpressibly affected. Found sobbing afterwards in own room. Quoted verses respecting self and young Gazelle. Ineffectually. Also referred to Patience on Monument. (Qy. Why on monument? J.M.)" (38:560). Julia has her final curtain bow in the last chapter, eternally quarreling with her "old Scotch Croesus"; but now the Desert of Sahara, the dried-up society around her, is only too real.

David's tyrannical landlady, Mrs. Crupp, is, again, a memorable comic voice, her best phrases in the tradition of Mrs. Gamp: " 'When the present set were took for you by your dear aunt, Mr. Copperfull,' said Mrs. Crupp, 'my remark were, I had now found summun I could care for. "Thank Ev'in!" were the expression, "I have now found summun I can care for!" ' Having discovered, rightly, from David's state that "there's a lady in the case," she issues her splendid warning: " 'It was but the gentleman which died here before yourself,' said Mrs. Crupp, 'that fell in love—with a barmaid—and had his waistcoats took in directly, though much swelled by drinking' " (26:398–99). When the "dear aunt" says she smelled of David's brandy and would trouble her to walk out, Mrs. Crupp threatens to bring both expressions "before a 'British Judy'—meaning, it was supposed, the bulwark of our national liberties." Like others of her tribe in Dickens, Mrs. Crupp has more to her: an ample nankeen bosom that needs constant soothing with brandy, an ability to make the most out of David's dinner parties for herself, and a vindictive jealousy of Peggotty that issues in her splendidly aggrieved letter to David and the laying of pitfalls for Peggotty on the stairs, in the hope of breaking her legs. But it is as a voice, falsely obsequious, self-dramatizing, that we most remember her.

Miss Mowcher, in the one comic scene Dickens was allowed for her, gives an unforgettable performance as well: "Ain't I volatile?" compensates, as a justified boast, for much that nature has denied her. She is very much more than a voice; for all her smallness she has a dynamic, dominating physical presence that makes her, in her one scene with Steerforth and David, one of the most formidable characters in the novel. She is highly intelligent and sees totally through the emptiness of the "society" she conjures up so brilliantly but recognizes just as keenly her need to live off it:

"Oh, my goodness, how polite we are!" exclaimed Miss Mowcher. . . . "What a world of gammon and spinach it is, though, ain't it!"

"What do you mean, Miss Mowcher," said Steerforth.

"Ha! ha! ha! What a refreshing set of humbugs we are, to be sure, ain't we, my sweet child?." . . . "Look here!" taking something out [of her bag]. "Scraps of the Russian Prince's nails. . . . The Prince's nails do more for me in private families of the genteel sort, than all my talents put together. I always carry 'em about. . . . Ha! ha! ha! Upon my life, 'the whole social system' (as the men call it when they make speeches in Parliament) is a system of Prince's nails!" (22:329–30)

Her sexual awareness is constantly suggestive: "Face like a peach," she says, pinching David's cheek as Steerforth introduces him to her. "Quite tempting! I'm very fond of peaches!" And a few minutes later, as she climbs up to the table: "'If either of you saw my ankles . . . say so, and I'll go home and destroy myself.' 'I did not,' said Steerforth. 'I did not,' said I. 'Well then,' cried Miss Mowcher, 'I'll consent to live'" (22:331).

It is not too far a cry to the sexual design—assistance to Steerforth in his planned seduction of little Emily—that is clearly the real purpose of her visit. By this time the repetition four times of her catchphrase "Ain't I volatile?" has achieved the sinister force Dickens obviously intended it to have.

Rosa Dartle, Mrs. Steerforth's companion, is anything but a comic figure; like Miss Wade of *Little Dorrit,* she is a self-tormentor, the victim, as David puts it on meeting her, of "some wasting fire within her." But her voice, her constant insinuation of her views, combined with a trick of questioning everything first, gives her a major impact. (This trick was taken, according to Forster, from "one of his lady friends, very familiar to him indeed" [556]—in fact, from Mrs. Brown, Angela Burdett-Coutts's companion and former governess.)[26] She uses it primarily—and successfully—to probe the set views of both Steerforth and his mother. On Oxford, for example: "'But isn't it, though?—I want to be put right, if I am wrong—isn't it, really?'

Voices

'Really what?' said Mrs. Steerforth. 'Oh! you mean it's *not!*' returned Miss Dartle. 'Well, I'm very glad to hear it! Now, I know what to do! That's the advantage of asking. I shall never allow people to talk before me about wastefulness and profligacy, and so forth, in connexion with that life, any more'" (20:293).

A few minutes later, she uses the same technique to expose the inhumanity of Steerforth's view of the Peggottys, "that sort of people." "'She brings,' said Steerforth, 'everything to a grindstone, and sharpens it. . . . She is all edge'" (294). A moment later we learn the motive for her sharpness with Steerforth and her self-torment: the scar on her lip, the result of his throwing a hammer at her, is cruel evidence of her youthful passion for him; she is much more than just physically damaged. It is this theme that informs one of the most remarkable scenes in the novel, the scene in Chapter 29 in which Steerforth, having softened Rosa with his charms, begs her to sing an Irish song, accompanying herself on her harp. She agrees, and sings passionately (in the manuscript the song was "The Last Rose of Summer," later canceled). Steerforth puts his arm "laughingly" about her and says, "Come, Rosa, for the future we will love each other very much!" She strikes him, throws him off "with the fury of a wild cat, and . . . burst out of the room" (29:435). The voice condemned here is not Rosa's but, for its inadequacy in response to her intense feelings, Steerforth's.

The scene of her violent rage with the returned little Emily in Chapter 50 will be discussed later (see Chapter 9); but in both its vindictiveness and its scornful mockery, hers is a voice that is never in control. Dickens's insight into Rosa's near-hysterical fury with the girl who had won Steerforth may be psychologically justified, but the scene of her singing—followed as it is by her violence—is incomparably better written.

Uriah Heep is grotesque rather than comic, and a major character in the novel. But he is inescapably a voice as well as a physical presence; both are odious. His "long, lank, skeleton hand" is the most unpleasant of the sensations the young David has on meeting him, and so clammy that David has to rub his own afterwards, to warm it, *and to rub his off*" (italics Dickens's).

63

The voice comes in the next chapter: "'I am well aware that I am the umblest person going,' said Uriah Heep, modestly; 'let the other be where he may. My mother is likewise a very umble person. We live in a numble abode, Master Copperfield, but have much to be thankful for. My father's former calling was umble. He was a sexton.' 'Where is he now?' I asked. 'He is a partaker of glory at present, Master Copperfield,' said Uriah Heep. 'But we have much to be thankful for'" (16:234–35).

It is all there: not only the repeated *umble,* which we shall hear many more times, but the rhythms of a particular kind of nonconformist hypocrisy that Dickens detested. "A partaker of glory at present" seems to assume that to claim his father's bliss as eternal would show pride, and the twice-repeated "we have much to be thankful for" accentuates his and his mother's modest gratitude.

The grasping of power beneath the paraded "umbleness" begins comically when Heep and his mother entertain the young David to tea: "A tender young cork . . . would have had no more chance against a pair of corkscrews, or a tender young tooth against a pair of dentists . . . than I had against Uriah and Mrs. Heep" (16:255). But as Heep's ascendancy over Wickfield grows, he becomes more and more threatening. One physical detail—as so often in Dickens—shows precisely what the Heep voice now signifies: "'If any one else had been in my place during the last few years, by this time he would have had Mr. Wickfield (oh, what a worthy man he is, Master Copperfield, too!) under his thumb. Un—der—his thumb,' said Uriah, very slowly, as he stretched out his cruel-looking hand above my table, and pressed his own thumb down upon it, until it shook, and shook the room" (25:379–80).

Uriah's sexual pursuit of Agnes is central to his character: there is something horrifying in his new voice of erotic desire, particularly in the image of the unripe pear he uses at the end of Chapter 39, after he has revolted Wickfield with his hopes: "'I suppose,' with a jerk, 'you have sometimes plucked a pear before it was ripe, Master Copperfield? . . . *I* did that last night,' said Uriah; 'but it'll ripen yet! It only wants attending to. I can wait!'" The passage ends: ". . . he made motions with his mouth as if the pear were ripe already, and he were smacking his lips over it" (580).

The responses Heep provokes from David, Betsey Trotwood, and, later, Micawber, constitute almost a new voice in themselves. Betsey's, after the news that she has lost her money, is the least surprising, since we know her directness already; but we hardly expect such a frontal attack, here on Heep's writhing and jerking about: "'Don't be galvanic, sir! . . . If you're an eel, sir, conduct yourself like one. If you're a man, control your limbs, sir! Good God!' said my aunt, with great indignation, 'I am not going to be serpentined and corkscrewed out of my senses!'" (35:517). David, hardly violent as a rule, has "a delirious idea of seizing the red-hot poker out of the fire, and running him through with it," when Heep confides to him his love for Agnes. Later, when he realizes that Heep has attempted to trap him into discussing his suspicions of Annie Strong, he loses all control and strikes Heep across the cheek ("I needed but the sound of his voice to be so madly enraged as I never was before, and never have been since" [42:619–20]).

The effect on Micawber of discovering and disclosing the villainy of Heep, his employer, is even more catastrophic. Micawber bursts into tears, breaks down in his attempt to make punch, and launches into a litany of what he will do to Heep. "'I'll put my hand in no man's hand,' said Mr. Micawber . . . 'until I have—blown to fragments—the—a—detestable—serpent—HEEP!'"; finally, he promises to crush "to—a—undiscoverable atoms—the—transcendent and immortal hypocrite and perjuror—HEEP!" (49:711). In Chapter 52 ("I assist at an Explosion") he keeps his word. This chapter is Micawber's *apogée* and will be discussed as such. But it is also the only scene in which we hear the true Heep voice; with the mask off, it is malicious, threatening, vindictive: "Now, come! I have got some of you under the harrow. Think twice, before it goes over you." "I am Shown Two Interesting penitents" gives us the old voice back again, but bolder in its pseudo-religious garb, more formalized, and, when we know the crime that has brought him to the model prison, more socially disturbing.

Both the Micawbers are pure, performing voices, recognizable at once in any place or situation; as comic voices, they buoy the novel up whenever it has most need. But they also have functions central to several of the novel's themes. On their first appearance, when the young David boards with them, they give him the only love and—for all their material plight—emotional security that London offers him; the kiss that Mrs. Micawber gives him as they leave for Plymouth is "just such," says David, "as she might have given to her own boy" (12:175). Quintessentially shabby-genteel themselves, they treat him as one of the family. They also treat him with profound courtesy and respect throughout the novel. In a bildungsroman they are the hero's friends who never cease to recognize his goodness. But they are also parodists, both of themselves and of almost all the pretensions in the novel. David's first impression, when he meets Micawber, is of "a certain condescending roll in his voice, and a certain indescribable air of doing something genteel," which impressed him very much. And neither Micawber is without condescension or gentility for the rest of the novel. Mrs. Micawber is particularly given to enumerating the branches of her family and to nostalgia for the time she lived with "papa and mama"; "experientia does it [instead of *docet* (teaches)]— as papa used to say," is a brilliant lapse. But Micawber also constantly deflates himself; his catchphrase, "in short," the deliberate slayer of his own rhetoric, is used three times in this first short meeting.

The main satirical target of Micawber's rhetoric is, of course, rhetoric itself—and particularly over-literary rhetoric, which Dickens loved to mock: "The blossom is blighted, the leaf is withered, the God of day goes down upon the dreary scene, and—and in short you are for ever floored. As I am!" (12:175). In the same way, the main target satirized in Micawber's endless letters is the literary pomposity of, particularly, public letter writing. But Dickens got it both ways: the parody is strongly there, but both the rhetorical speeches and the letters are a delight to read.

Micawber's financial misfortunes and his wife's comments on them provide another running comic commentary: on the world of commerce. Mrs. Micawber's strictures on both the Custom House in Plymouth and the Medway Coal Trade are extremely funny, but they also bring us nearer the heart of both those institutions than the little we learn about export and import in *Dombey and Son*. On the Custom House: "'The truth is, talent is not wanted in the Custom House,' said Mrs. Micawber. 'They would rather *not* have a man of Mr. Micawber's abilities. He would only show the deficiency of the others.'" And on the Medway Coal Trade: "'We came,' repeated Mrs. Micawber, 'and saw the Medway. My opinion of the coal trade on that river is, that it may require talent, but that it certainly requires capital. Talent, Mr. Micawber has,—capital, Mr. Micawber has not. We saw, I think, the greater part of the Medway; and that is my individual conclusion'" (17:259–60).

, One major human weakness that the Micawber comedy parodies is the over-romanticism of David—the ultimate cause of his "undisciplined heart"—and the much more dangerous protean volatility of Steerforth, which David naively admires. In the Micawbers it is caricatured as a kind of "elasticity," a remarkably swift recovery after the depths of gloom. Micawber's first letter to David, after their convivial night at Canterbury, sets the pattern: "The die is cast—all is over," it begins; and "this is the last communication . . . you will ever receive . . . From / The / Beggared Outcast / WILKINS MICAWBER," it ends (17:263).

The panic-stricken David, still a schoolboy, runs at once to offer Micawber comfort but finds him, on the London coach, "the very picture of tranquil enjoyment . . . eating walnuts out of a paper bag, with a bottle sticking out of his breast pocket" (17:264).

Mrs. Micawber is quite capable of similar recoveries herself: "I have known her," says David, "to be thrown into fainting fits by the king's taxes at three o'clock, and to eat lamb-chops breaded, and drink warm ale (paid for with two tea-spoons that had gone to the pawnbroker's) at four (11:159).

The last chapters of the novel are marked by a succession of such violent changes of mood; Micawber alternately despairs as Heep's writs are served on him and rises to earthly bliss as Traddles pays his debts. Only as the emigrant ship leaves the Thames can Micawber, now very much a settler, sail securely to his Australian triumphs.

But before that, he has had his scene of triumph in England: his exposure of Heep's villainy as Wickfield's partner in Canterbury (Chapter 52). It is done, of course, by letter, which he reads out with immense enjoyment to the assembled company, a letter that not only castigates the name "Heep" throughout but sandwiches it between quotations from *Hamlet* (read twice) and Nelson. It is his supreme theatrical performance, superbly prepared and stage-managed by himself. Even his large office-ruler plays its part, as both stage effect and weapon, by disabling Heep's right hand when he attempts to seize the letter. It is a devastating exposé and intensely satisfying as the end of the Heep subplot. The new Heep voice of snarling fury, once the mask of humility has been dropped, has already been commented on; but Dickens could not resist giving him one riposte of genuine comic force: "You know what *I* want?" says Betsey Trotwood, who has seized Heep by the collar, to force him to return the money he has swindled her out of. "A strait-waistcoat," says Heep (52:758).

But the scene is essentially Micawber's; it is followed by the touching scene of reconciliation with Mrs. Micawber and a list of what they can now expect, declaimed with all of Micawber's old enjoyment: "'Now, welcome poverty!' cried Mr. Micawber, shedding tears. 'Welcome misery, welcome houselessness, welcome hunger, rags, tempest, and beggary! Mutual confidence will sustain us to the end!'" (52:761).

Chapter Seven

Marriage

David's sudden questioning of Peggotty about marriage, when he is a very young boy (in Chapter 2)—and particularly about widows remarrying—has its obvious place in the novel as an ironical foretaste of the future. But besides that, it hints strongly that marriage will be a key theme of the book. There are few Dickens novels, indeed, in which there are so many marriages, so different from each other, and probed with such understanding.

Clara Copperfield's two marriages are, of course, vital to the whole story. The first has clearly been happy, if unworldly. Betsey Trotwood sums up her nephew, the first David Copperfield, as someone "who was always running after wax dolls from his cradle," but she had obviously loved him. Before she meets Murdstone, she sums up both him and the all-too-vulnerable Clara: "a mighty pleasure for the poor Baby to fix her simple faith upon any dog of a fellow, certain to ill-use her in some way or other" (13:196). We are shown the full destructive effects of the Murdstones' self-proclaimed "firmness" on Clara as well as on David, of the metallic sister's dominating position in the household, and of their joint determination to kill any demonstration of love for David in his mother. Although Peggotty concedes that Clara loves her husband, this is a gloomy caricature of a marriage. It is Betsey Trotwood, again, who, without mincing her words, accuses Murdstone of virtually murdering his wife: "And when you had made sure of the poor little fool . . . because you had not done wrong enough to her and hers, you must begin to train her, must you? begin to break her, like a poor caged bird, and wear her deluded life away, in teaching her to sing *your* notes? . . . You were a tyrant to the simple baby, and you broke her heart" (14:213).

Mr. Chillip's comments to David (inspired by Mrs. Chillip) on Murdstone's second marriage—again to a young woman of beauty and property—are even stronger than Betsey Trotwood's on the first: "Tyranny, gloom, and worry have made Mrs. Murdstone nearly imbecile. She was a lively young woman, sir, before marriage, and their gloom and austerity destroyed her. They go about with her, now, more like her keepers than her husband and sister-in-law" (59:833–34). That picture of what the Murdstone temperament could do to a young wife is one of the harshest comments on marriage in a Dickens novel.

It is offset by the innocent comicality of Barkis's wooing of Peggotty—and by its ultimate success. Catchphrases play their comic part here: "Barkis is willin'" and "Are you pretty comfortable?" As do his presents: "a double set of pigs' trotters, a huge pin-cushion, half a bushel or so of apples," and many more. "I have often thought, since, what an odd, innocent, out-of-the-way kind of wedding it must have been!" says David, after he and little Emily have been their only companions on their drive to the church (10:147). But the marriage of Barkis and Peggotty is not only comic; Dickens presents it as an entirely affectionate marriage on both sides. Barkis's "nearness" over money and the box under his bed where he keeps it are presented more comically than otherwise; but his death is done with great care and dignity: "'Barkis, my dear!' said Peggotty. 'C. P. Barkis,' he cried faintly. 'No better woman anywhere!' 'Look! Here's Master Davy!' said Peggotty. For he now opened his eyes. I was on the point of asking him if he knew me, when he tried to stretch out his arm, and said to me, distinctly, with a pleasant smile: 'Barkis is willin'!' And, it being low water, he went out with the tide" (30:445).

Marriage

We see Betsey Trotwood's mysterious husband only once, apart from his sudden eruption near St. Paul's to obtain money from her and her telling David of his death. Like Compeyson in *Great Expectations*, he has made away with her fortune and nearly broken her heart; but unlike Miss Havisham, Betsey has survived as a strongly positive presence, if embittered about marriage. Dickens, in fact, treated comically here what becomes tragic in Miss Havisham: "Janet [Betsey's maid] . . . was one of a series of protégées whom my aunt had taken into her service expressly to educate in a renouncement of mankind, and who had generally completed their abjuration by marrying the baker" (13:194). But what she tells David, who comes upon him when her husband is again obtaining money from her, justifies her anxieties about his marriage; she too, as she freely admits to him, has been "blind! blind! blind!" " 'He was a fine-looking man when I married him,' said my aunt . . . 'and I believed him—I was a fool!—to be the soul of honour! . . . I was in earnest, Trot, if ever a woman was' " (47:689).

He may be a melodramatic figure in the background ("an adventurer, a gambler, and a cheat") and the marriage only a disaster in the past. But it has its place in the novel as another instance of the "undisciplined heart," and its effects on Betsey Trotwood are highly important.

To the subplot involving Dr. Strong, his young wife Annie, her cousin Jack Maldon, and her mother, Mrs. Markleham ("the Old Soldier"), Dickens devotes three chapters, as well as other mentions. He also involves Uriah Heep and, as its triumphant unraveler, Mr. Dick. Dickens gave one of his purposes in his chapter summary for Chapter 45 ("Mr. Dick fulfils my Aunt's Predictions"): "Shew faults of mothers, and their consequences." The "faults of mothers" are shown only too clearly in "the Old Soldier," with her constant importuning of her daughter to beg favors from her husband. As Betsey Trotwood puts it: "There never would have been anything the matter if it hadn't been for that old Animal. . . . It's very much to be wished that some mothers would leave their daughters alone after marriage, and not be so violently affectionate" (45:663).

Betsey's sotto voce asides to "the Old Soldier" give, in fact, some much-needed comic relief to the long, drawn-out rhetoric of Annie's final "confession." To explore the difficulties of a marriage between an old scholar and a beautiful young woman was in itself a bold stroke, although one done by George Eliot with her Casaubon and Dorothea in *Middlemarch,* twenty years later, much more impressively. But both Annie and the Doctor are too good to be true, and the language they use has the peculiar deadness of self-indulgent rhetoric. "It only remains for me to bear the knowledge of the unhappiness I have occasioned, as submissively as I can. It is she who should reproach; not I," says the Doctor, in his guilt over marrying Annie at all. And Annie, when she has satisfactorily explained everything, "Oh, take me to your heart, my husband, for my love was founded on a rock, and it endures" (45:663). David's description of her look, on the night after Jack Maldon has departed for India, almost suggests real guilt: "It was so fixed in its abstraction, it was so full of a wild, sleep-walking, dreamy horror of I don't know what. . . . Penitence, humiliation, shame, pride, love, and trustfulness, I see them all; and in them all, I see that horror of I don't know what" (16:246). But there is no indication in the number plans that Dickens had ever considered the commission of any real wrong, and Annie's character from the beginning makes it impossible. The gap, in fact, between the only indiscretion we are shown—giving the departing Jack Maldon a ribbon—and the intensity of her self-incrimination is, with the over-heightened language, a major reason why the subplot is so unconvincing.

The Micawbers share with the Traddleses (though the Traddleses only achieve it at the end of the novel) the most successful marriage we are shown. Whatever their pecuniary difficulties, they remain a totally united family. We see only one quarrel—caused by Micawber's desperate state in working for Heep—and that ends in a marvelously complete reconciliation scene, with husband and wife folded in each other's embrace. There is little need for Mrs. Micawber to repeat "I never will desert Mr. Micawber"; it is inconceivable that she should ever do so. Mrs. Micawber's chief memory of their wedding ceremony may be of reading the service over "with a flat-candle" the previous night; but whatever the legal bond, they are perfectly attuned to each other, in their fantasies, their language, their extraordinary ability either to ignore or to surmount all obstacles. Their devotion to each other—as demonstrative as everything else about them—reduces David to tears: " 'Emma, my angel!' cried Mr. Micawber, running into the room; 'what is the matter?' 'I never will desert you, Micawber!' she exclaimed. 'My life!' said Mr. Micawber, taking her in his arms. 'I am perfectly aware of it.' 'He is the parent of my children! He is the father of my twins! He is the husband of my affections,' cried Mrs. Micawber, struggling; 'and I ne—ver—will—desert Mr. Micawber!' " (12:172).

Mrs. Micawber's pride in her husband's talents is limitless and gives us a succession of splendid commercial fantasies: the Custom House, the Medway Coal Trade, brewing, banking—all are grist to her mill. But her real triumph as a wife is to persuade Micawber to assert himself, to "throw down the gauntlet to society, and say, in effect, "Show me who will take that up. Let the party immediately step forward' " (28:419). As we know, Uriah Heep steps forward; for all the heart-burnings it leads to for both Micawbers, it is, before Micawber's success in Australia, the only thing that "turns up" for him. Even then, Mrs. Micawber has to be reassured that such a subordinate post as Heep's confidential clerk will not spoil Micawber's chances of rising to the top of the legal profession. " 'Now, for example, Mr. Traddles,' said Mrs. Micawber, assuming a profound air, 'a Judge, or even say a Chancellor. Does an individual place himself beyond the pale of those preferments by entering on such an office as Mr. Micawber has accepted?' " (36:533). Fantasy—but totally loyal fantasy—can scarcely go further, after what we have seen and heard of Micawber.

Although not such an avid letter-writer as her husband, Mrs. Micawber, in the two letters she writes (to David and Traddles) about the terrible effects on Micawber of working for Heep, shows that she can well rival him. And her despair is as a wife and mother. For herself, only circumlocution will do: "In general, Mr. Micawber has had no secrets from the bosom of affection—I allude to his wife"; and a few lines later: "He is reserved. He is secret. His life is a mystery to the partner of his joys and sorrows—I again allude to his wife" (42:624).

Writing about the family (to Traddles now), she can dramatize the telling detail: "Last night, on being childishly solicited for two-pence, to buy 'lemon-stunners'—a local sweetmeat—he presented an oyster-knife at the twins!" (49:703–4).

Near the end of the novel the whole Micawber family, dramatically dressed for the voyage, united and confident in a new way, only await the emigration ship; Mrs. Micawber, in her belief in her husband's destiny, is at her very best: "'My dear Mr. Copperfield,' said Mrs. Micawber, 'I wish Mr. Micawber to feel his position. . . . I wish Mr. Micawber to take his stand upon that vessel's prow, and firmly say, "This country I am come to conquer! Have you honours? Have you riches? Have you posts of profitable pecuniary emolument? Let them be brought forward. They are mine!" . . . I wish Mr. Micawber . . . to be the Caesar of his own fortunes'" (57:808).

Fantasy again, no doubt; but, as David says, her conviction "gave a moral elevation to her tone which I think I had never heard in it before." And it perhaps makes Micawber's elevation to the magistracy just a shade less improbable.

From his first appearance at Salem House, drawing skeletons and backing up Mr. Mell against Steerforth, Tommy Traddles, simple-hearted, generous, and amiable, is perhaps the most attractive character in the novel. And his marriage to Sophy, "the dearest girl in the world," for which he has to wait until Chapter 59, is certainly the happiest. For most of the novel we see him stoically waiting, full of sympathy for Sophy's father, the ill-paid Rev. Horace Crewler, her invalid mother, and her regiment of sisters, down in Devonshire. So that, when David returns from Switzerland to find Traddles at last married, we expect him to be justly rewarded. The description of Sophy and five of her sisters, "a perfect nest of roses," secreted away by day and romping at night, in Traddles's Gray's Inn chambers, is indeed paradisal and made the more so by its contrast with the drab legal world surrounding it. "The society of girls," says Traddles, "is a very delightful thing, Copperfield. It's not professional, but it's very delightful."' The episode is capped with an allusion to one of Dickens's favorite *Arabian Nights* tales: the presence of the Devonshire girls "in that grim atmosphere of pounce and parchment, red-tape" and all the rest of it "seemed almost as pleasantly fanciful as if I had dreamed that the

Sultan's famous family had been admitted on the roll of attorneys, and had brought the talking bird, the singing tree, and the golden water into Gray's Inn Hall" (59:830).

"I believe you make yourselves, and each other, two of the happiest people in the world," says David, when he meets Traddles once more, and the last we hear of Traddles is that he is well on the way to becoming a judge and he and Sophy are living—with more of the girls—in one of the houses they had imagined as their home in their evening walks of long before. Michael Slater, in *Dickens and Women* (83–84), is surely right in seeing as the inspiration for the idyllic scene in Traddles's Gray's Inn chambers, Dickens's memories of Mary Hogarth, Catherine's younger sister, living with them after their marriage in Furnival's Inn.

David's marriage to Dora is, of course, the central marriage of the novel, and the scenes describing it some of the most delightful. Dickens manages to criticize both partners—David for his over-romanticism, Dora for her childish fecklessness—without robbing them of their charm. A light, affectionate comedy plays over Dora's world: Jip in his Chinese Pagoda, her aunts Clarissa and Lavinia, who "treat her a little too much like a plaything," her self-dramatizing bosom friend, Julia Mills. The accounts of her housekeeping—particularly their first "little dinner" for Traddles—and of their impossible servants are marvelously funny, as are her responses to David's criticisms: " 'My sweet, I am only going to reason.' 'Oh, but reasoning is worse than scolding!' exclaims Dora, in despair. 'I didn't marry to be reasoned with.' " And when David tells her they are spoiling the servants, especially their page, now transported for stealing a gold watch, she exclaims, " 'You said I hadn't turned out well, and compared me to him.' 'To whom?' I asked. 'To the page,' sobbed Dora. 'Oh, you cruel fellow, to compare your affectionate wife to a transported page! Why didn't you tell me your opinion of me before we were married?' " (48:693).

But under this comically pettish surface there are deeper criticisms: "The old unhappy loss or want of something had, I am conscious, some place in my heart. . . . I could have wished my wife had been my counsellor. . . . Thus it was that I took upon myself the toils and cares of our life, and had no partner in them" (44:646). Four chapters later, David, in a long passage of self-analysis, uses these same terms as he probes into himself again; we feel strongly that this is a further extension of autobiography.

Two things keep these anxieties at bay: Dora's instinctive awareness of her own limitations and Betsey Trotwood's more mature wisdom. Dora's request that David think of her as his "child-wife" has a tenderness and seriousness of implication that David grasps at the time, above all, the implication that he should accept her as she is and not as he would like her to be: "When you miss what I should like to be, and I think can never be, say, 'still my foolish child-wife loves me!' For indeed I do." It also leads on to David's ultimate realization that his plan to "form" Dora's mind—another way of changing her—was doomed to failure: "I found myself in the condition of a schoolmaster, a trap, a pitfall; of always playing spider to Dora's fly, and always pouncing out of my hole to her infinite disturbance. . . . It began to occur to me that perhaps Dora's mind was already formed" (48:695).

Betsey's wisdom reflects both her fondness for them and the lessons of her own past; her realism is founded in experience. When David asks her to "counsel" Dora a little, she reminds him sharply of the dangers of meddling: "I want our pet to like me, and be as gay as a butterfly. Remember your own home, in that second marriage; and never do both me and her the injury you have hinted at!" (44:638). And a few lines later, in words that have a peculiarly modern ring: "But remember, my dear, your future is between you two. No one can assist you; you are to work it out for yourselves. This is marriage, Trot" (44:639).

This is the more generous in Betsey since it is made clear throughout that Agnes was her choice for David. Indeed, before meeting Dora, her questions about her are needling enough: " 'Not silly?' said my aunt. . . . 'Not light-hearted?' said my aunt." Her twice-repeated "blind, blind, blind!" anticipates what is weakest in the marriage; David's response, "and without knowing why, I felt a vague unhappy, loss or want of something overshadow me like a cloud" (35:504), anticipates again—in virtually the same words—the probing analysis of his marriage in Chapter 44.

Marriage

The ultimate marriage between David and Agnes does not take place until Chapter 62, but it is clearly planned from their first meeting in Chapter 15. A major disappointment in her, as heroine of a love story, is that she does not develop. Her "sisterly," "good angel" qualities—her ever "pointing upward," the "tranquil brightness" of "a stained glass window in a church"—are what impress the young David at once, and they continue to impress him throughout the novel. Like David, we incline to take her for granted. Both her sympathies and her antipathies are always right: her devotion to her father, her affection for Dora; her suspicions of Steerforth, her fear of Uriah. But she is never allowed the liveliness of Dora, and, above all—in a novel in which so much of the life springs from comedy—she is never allowed to be comic. A major reason for this, of course, is that her dominant inspiration was Mary Hogarth; but this was the Mary sanctified after her early death—not the Mary whose living with the newly married Dickenses may have helped to inspire the Traddles chapter.

Comedy barred, the disclosure of their love for each other—hidden by Agnes, unrecognized by David—is allowed some rather clumsy irony to help it along: Betsey Trotwood's "pious fraud," first, that Agnes has "an attachment," and secondly, that she is going to be married. The disclosure itself takes two chapters, Chapters 60 and 62; David's parting remark to Agnes in Chapter 60 has a clearly ironic force—particularly when we remember Agnes's heroically successful concealment: "I felt . . . that you could be faithfully affectionate against all discouragement, and never cease to be so, until you ceased to live. —Will you laugh at such a dream?" (60:844).

Agnes's two remarks to David in Chapter 62 in a sense bind the novel together: "I have loved you all my life!" and the fulfillment of Dora's last charge to her, "That only I would occupy this vacant place." Both appear in the number plans; they were clearly of great importance to Dickens.

The marriage itself is not described; it is simply part of the mellow, pastoral end of the novel: "I had advanced in fame and fortune, my domestic joy was perfect, I had been married ten happy years" (63:866).

Chapter Eight
Parents, Children, and Orphans

Many of the heroes of the bildungsroman are orphans, and it is easy to see why. The orphan as a child commands instant pity in his or her need of security and love; the achievement of both, by the end of the novel, thus becomes both more dramatic and more pleasure-giving. Both of Dickens's bildungsroman heroes, David and Pip, are virtually orphans: Pip from the beginning of his story, David with the death of his mother when he is still a schoolboy. But it is remarkable how many other characters of *David Copperfield* are either orphans or have lost one parent. The first list would include little Emily, Ham, David's mother, and Rosa Dartle; the second, Steerforth, Agnes, Dora, Annie Strong, and Uriah Heep. George Ford, the first to make this point, notes, too, Freud's admiration of the novel and the obvious attraction to him of its "preoccupation with children in relation to fathers and mothers."[27]

Dickens was intensely interested in familial relationships—including their obverse, orphanhood, and its often damaging effects—in all his novels, particularly, perhaps, in the five that fill the decade from 1846 to 1856: *Dombey and Son, David Copperfield, Bleak House,*

Parents, Children, and Orphans

Hard Times, and *Little Dorrit*. Florence Dombey's relationship with her father, Louise Gradgrind's with hers, and Amy's relationship with William Dorrit, show an increasing awareness of unsatisfactory fathers and the pain they cause to their children.

In *David Copperfield* the effects are more varied and in some ways just as psychologically challenging. David himself, as a virtual orphan after his mother's remarriage, suffers intensely until he is rescued by Betsey Trotwood. His "undisciplined heart" as a young man, both in his continued hero worship of Steerforth and his "blind" love of Dora, is clearly intimately connected with his need for love and security as an orphan. With all her difference in class and background—and, above all, in being happily brought up by a doting uncle—little Emily shares something of the same psychological pattern (and we know how Dickens loved patterns, the more esoteric the better) in her easy conquest by Steerforth. Steerforth himself, brought up by an over-possessive mother and her companion, who adores him, explicitly blames his lack of a father for his sensual weakness and irresponsibility in his pursuit of Emily: "David, I wish to God I had had a judicious father these last twenty years!" (22:322).

The other characters in *David Copperfield* who have lost one parent respond to their situations in very different ways. The most intense study is of Annie Strong, brought up, like Steerforth, by a possessive and interfering mother; but totally unlike Steerforth, she is wracked by guilt and remorse for what she tortures herself into seeing as an offense against her father-figure husband. By showing how far she is above the libertine Jack Maldon in every possible way—in sensibility, delicacy, unselfishness—and what a disaster marriage to him would have been, Dickens creates a powerful study in the irrationality of guilt. Uriah Heep is discussed elsewhere both as a grotesque figure of black comedy and as an emblem of evil. But it is important to remember that, however much his father, now "a partaker of glory," instilled into him the importance of "umbleness," it is his mother who has brought him up, and it is her indulgence that lies behind his thirst for money, power, and sexual gratification.

Dora, too, has only one parent in the novel, her fond and vain father; indeed, for half of the novel, she is an orphan. Her most conspicuous faults—impracticality, light-headedness, pettishness—are relatively minor ones, and fully compensated for by her genuine love for David and her feminine attractiveness. But her self-indulgence is more than minor, and David is forced to admit to himself her inadequacy as a wife. In both her attractiveness and her faults she bears a strong resemblance to David's mother (an important part of her attraction for David), and we remember that David's mother was also an orphan.

Rosa Dartle, as a haunting presence in the novel, is important enough to merit a section of her own (see Chapter 9). She is, with Miss Wade and Mrs. Clennan, one of what Angus Wilson has aptly called "clinical studies that must demand the Freudian's admiration."[28] Dickens's insight here is into the perverse forms of hatred and virtual sadism born of her dependence on Mrs. Steerforth and her frustrated passion for Steerforth himself; behind both her dependence and her need for love—destroyed as it is by Steerforth—lies her orphanhood.

Orphans and children denied one parent in their upbringing are often in acute, if subconscious, need of surrogate parents; no Dickens novel has more of these, of a more varied kind, than *David Copperfield*. David himself has to undergo, first, the horrors of the Murdstones as ghastly parodies of surrogates, then the creation as a father-figure of the ultimately despicable Steerforth (and the fact that, even after the seduction of Emily, he never loses David's love is a brilliant insight into the power of need). The Micawbers, for all their comically displayed unreliability, offer him parental affection when he most desperately needs it; but it is, of course, Betsey Trotwood, supported by Mr. Dick, who, in the love and security they give him from his arrival in Dover onwards, become his true parents. Besides them, and gradually—and importantly—united with them, and especially with Betsey, is Peggotty who, after David's mother's death, is treated by him as a near mother-figure: "From that night there grew up in my breast a feeling for Peggotty which I cannot very well define. She did not replace my mother; no one could do that; but she came into a vacancy in my heart, which closed upon her, and I felt towards her something I have never felt for any other human being" (61).

But the surrogate father par excellence throughout the novel is Daniel Peggotty; treated as a father by the two orphans, Ham and Emily, he has brought up, they are as devoted to him as he to them. Daniel Peggotty is Mrs. Gummidge's compassionate and patient protector, and the creator of the most vividly realized home in the novel. One of the cruelest ironies in *David Copperfield* is that Daniel Peggotty suffers the most palpably. It is as a father that he sets out to seek the fallen Emily through the world; it is to try and save this virtual daughter's grief that he keeps the news of Ham's death from her for a year in Australia.

In the essay "Dickens: A Haunting," from which I have already quoted, Angus Wilson finds the source of much of the haunting in the ambiguities inherent in Dickens's treatment of "the home" and "the wanderer": the home could also be a prison, the wanderer could be bent on evil or on escape from evil. *David Copperfield* has full measure of both, at times haunting enough. The wandering of the orphaned hero from a prison disguised as a home, through the surrogate homes of Dover and marriage with Dora, to the genuine home he creates at the end with Agnes, makes the novel as much an exploration into familial relationships—and particularly of parents and children—as a traditional bildungsroman.

Chapter Nine

Rosa Dartle: The History of a "Self-Tormentor"

Dickens's most impressive study of a "self-tormentor," as he there called her, came in *Little Dorrit*, six years after *David Copperfield*, in Miss Wade's written narrative about her past. As an orphan and a governess, with a sharp intelligence but an "unhappy temper," she bitterly resents what she sees as patronage everywhere; this barely suppressed resentment governs her actions and character. Rosa Dartle is also a self-tormentor, but her resentments are different; they are focused on her frustrated passion for Steerforth and on his mother's possessiveness over him. She shares both Miss Wade's sharp intelligence and her unhappy temper. But there is one essential difference between them, which mirrors both the very different kinds of novel *David Copperfield* and *Little Dorrit* are and the remarkable density and interconnectedness of the latter. "In Miss Wade," Dickens told Forster, "I had an idea which I thought a new one, of making the introduced story [her virtual abduction of Tattycoram] so fit into surroundings impossible of separation from the main story, as to make the blood of the book circulate through both" (Forster, 626). Dickens made no attempt to do this with Rosa Dartle, but the scenes of her frustration, fury, and intense jealousy are still strikingly powerful.

Rosa Dartle

The hammer scar on her upper lip—the legacy of her passion for Steerforth—and her violent striking of him after singing and playing on her harp have been discussed already, as have her notable linguistic oddities (see Chapter 6). What motivates her for the rest of the novel is her violent jealousy: first, of little Emily, and then, after Steerforth's death, of his mother and what she characterizes as her "corrupt" influence over him.

In a sense, Rosa Dartle is framed by the scar. It dominates her first appearance in Chapter 20, and Steerforth tells its story with an almost brutal terseness: "I was a young boy, and she exasperated me, and I threw a hammer at her" (295). For David, the scar is the most compelling thing about her; when her portrait looks down on him at night, he has to insert it: "The painter hadn't made the scar, but I made it" (298). And it dominates her to the last; in Chapter 56, David reports Steerforth's death to his mother and Rosa: "'Aye!' cried Rosa, smiting herself passionately on the breast, 'look at me! Moan, and groan, and look at me! Look here!' striking the scar, 'at your dead child's handiwork!'" (799).

But in between, it is on Steerforth's new love that her jealousy focuses; long before we know of his designs on little Emily, she shows the suspicions of a naturally—or unnaturally—jealous woman: "'What is he doing?' she said with an eagerness that seemed enough to consume her like a fire. 'In what is that man [Littimer] assisting him, who never looks at me without an inscrutable falsehood in his eyes? If you are honourable and faithful, I don't ask you to betray your friend. I ask you only to tell me, is it anger, is it hatred, is it pride, is it restlessness, is it some wild fancy, is it love, *what is it*, that is leading him?'" (29:432).

Some commentators have said that Dickens rarely depicted sexual passion convincingly. But the passion of fury that seizes Rosa Dartle, when she learns of little Emily's elopement with Steerforth, is the black obverse of sexual passion—the verbal revenge of a woman once scorned, now confronted with the triumph of a rival. The difference in class, as Dickens unerringly knew, drives her almost to madness: "'They are a depraved, worthless set. I would have her whipped . . . I would trample on them all. . . . I would have his house pulled down.

I would have her branded on the face, drest in rags, and cast out in the streets to starve'" (32:471).

When David next sees her, as they hear Littimer's intelligence of how Steerforth has abandoned little Emily in Naples, she is much more controlled; but it is a control buoyed by the hope that Emily may be dead. As she gives it utterance, the "vaunting cruelty with which she met my glance," says David, "I never saw expressed in any other face that ever I have seen" (46:667).

Four chapters later, we have the culmination of Rosa Dartle's rage and scorn in her all but physical flaying of Emily in London. For sheer vindictiveness, it is probably unrivaled in Dickens; it is clear that the earlier scenes of her passionate resentment are only a prelude to it. But here it is difficult not to be uneasy: the rhetoric is too strained, as if Dickens was deliberately experimenting with how far such vehement language can go; and Emily's pitiful responses are peculiarly dead. The whole scene teeters on the edge of melodrama—or goes over it. It is only when Rosa's rage turns to mockery that we fully believe again in this study of a totally thwarted woman:

"'*She* love!' she said. 'That carrion! And he ever cared for her, she'd tell me. Ha, ha! The little liars that these traders are!'" (50:721).

Her frenzied upbraiding of Mrs. Steerforth, on David's bringing the news of her son's death, is more terrible: first, because we know that most of what she says is true and cruelly penetrating; secondly, because of when she says it; and thirdly, because it is met not by dead rhetoric but by the moans of a bereaved mother. And for the first time she unbares all the self-torment that has driven her: "'Have I been silent all these years, and shall I not speak now? I loved him better than you ever loved him!' turning on her fiercely. 'I could have loved him, and asked no return. If I had been his wife, I could have been the slave of his caprices for a word of love a year. I should have been. Who knows it better than I? You were exacting, proud, punctilious, selfish. My love would have been devoted—would have trod your paltry whimpering under foot!'" (56:800).

Mrs. Steerforth herself is a remarkable study in pride and pain, and again, as with Rosa Dartle's scar, it is the physical details that tell us most:

Rosa Dartle

"The moan the mother uttered, from time to time, went to my heart. Always the same. Always inarticulate and stifled. Always accompanied with an incapable motion of the head, but with no change of face. Always proceeding from a rigid mouth and closed teeth, as if the jaw were locked and the face frozen up in pain" (56:799).

The final vignette of them—Mrs. Steerforth wandering in her mind, Rosa Dartle alternately caressing and quarreling with her, both still obsessed with the dead Steerforth—is as melancholy as anything in Dickens: "Thus I leave them; thus I always find them; thus they wear their time away, from year to year" (64:875).

The two pentameters are a sufficient index of Dickens's emotional involvement in this part of the story.

Chapter Ten
Social Criticism

David Copperfield follows a novel fully engaged with society. The full title of Dombey and Son—*Dealings with the Firm of Dombey and Son, Wholesale, Retail, and for Exportation*—shows its concern with money and business; Dombey himself, his second marriage, and the novel's two schools, Doctor Blimber's exclusive establishment in Brighton and, contrasted with it, the Charitable Grinders, where boys are taught to keep to their station in life, show its concern with class.

Of the two schools we are shown in *Copperfield*, Dr. Strong's in Canterbury is largely there to show up the appallingness of Salem House, just as the scholarly (if not over-effective) Dr. Strong himself shows up the coarse ignorance of Mr. Creakle. Class prejudice (or money prejudice) is exposed in the dismissal of Mr. Mell because his mother lives on charity in an almshouse; but class as such was not Dickens's main target, as it had been in *Dombey*. His target here was the caricature of education offered by a once bankrupt hop-dealer, ignorant of anything except "the art of slashing" (Steerforth's description seems entirely justified). It is Dickens the social critic and passionate believer in education who stands behind David's judgment on

Creakle: "I am sure when I think of the fellow now, my blood rises against him with the disinterested indignation I should feel if I could have known all about him without having ever been in his power; but it rises hotly, because I know him to have been an incapable brute, who had no more right to be possessed of the great trust he held, than to be Lord High Admiral, or Commander-in-Chief—in either of which capacities it is probable that he would have done infinitely less mischief" (7:90).

But two other schools are mentioned, both by Uriah Heep to David: the foundation school for boys, at which both he and his father had been brought up, and his mother's "public, sort of charitable, establishment." Their aims are clearly similar to those of the Charitable Grinders: "They taught us all a deal of umbleness—not much else that I know of, from morning to night." It is impossible to overestimate the effect of this schooling on Heep; Dickens, talking again through David, made his own vehement criticism of such schools quite clear: "It was the first time it had ever occurred to me, that this detestable cant of false humility might have originated out of the Heep family. I had seen the harvest, but had never thought of the seed" (39:575).

Law, in the form of Doctors' Commons, is another of Dickens's social targets. He presents it with little, if any, of the voracity and corruption of Chancery in *Bleak House*; but the satire is considerably sharper than in the sketch "Doctors' Commons" in *Sketches by Boz*. Ridicule of the bewildering mixture of cases administered by ecclesiastical law in the many Commons courts—wills, marriages, divorces, collisions at sea—is common to both, but the picture here is of excessive gentility, vanity, muddle, and greed. Most of the ridicule is centered on Mr. Spenlow, David's employer, with his belief in the proctor's profession as "the genteelest profession in the world"; on his sheltering behind the mild Mr. Jorkins whenever he is faced with a difficult decision; and on his absurd catchphrase, "Touch the Commons, and down comes the country!" It is appropriate that, after his defense of the chaotic keeping of wills in the Prerogative Office, warmly attacked by David (and one of Dickens's bête-noires), he is found, on his death, to have left no will himself. It is appropriate, too, that the last glimpse

we have of Doctors' Commons is the highly undignified one of out-
siders touting for work there.

Both Salem House and Doctors' Commons play their part in David's fortunes; but Dickens's criticism of both is hardly germane to any
underlying theme in the novel. This is not the case with his treatment
of little Emily, the "fallen" girl, and Martha Endell, the prostitute.
Writing to his friend William de Cerjat on 29 December 1849, about
halfway through the novel, Dickens made clear his sympathy for little
Emily: "I had previously observed much of what you say about the
poor girls. In all you suggest with so much feeling of their return to
virtue being cruelly cut off, I concur with a sore heart. I have been
turning it over in my mind for some time, and hope, in the history of
Little Em'ly (who *must* fall—there is no hope for her) to put it before
the thoughts of people, in a new and pathetic way, and perhaps to do
some good" (*Letters* 5:682).

The treatment of Martha shows that his sympathy extended to
prostitutes, too. Much of this feeling came undoubtedly from his running of the Home for Fallen Women for Angela Burdett-Coutts. But
whereas in his stream of letters to her about the girls he was lively—
often racy—in the extreme, his dealing with the fates of both Little
Emily and Martha was constricted by conventional and often dead-
ening rhetoric. One example is little Emily's letter to Ham, left for him
on her elopement: "Oh, if you knew how my heart is torn. If even
you, that I have wronged so much, that never can forgive me, could
only know what I suffer! I am too wicked to write about myself. Oh,
take comfort in thinking that I am so bad. Oh, for mercy's sake, tell
uncle that I never loved him half so dear as now" (31:452). And so
on, in the same vein.

Another is Martha's outburst, tempted to throw herself into the
Thames: "'Oh, the river!' she cried passionately. 'Oh, the river! . . . I
know it's like me!' she exclaimed. 'I know that I belong to it. I know
that it's the natural company of such as I am!'" (47:681). And so on,
again.

Both little Emily and Martha have their better moments, of
course. Little Emily's fury when Steerforth deserts her in Naples (as

described by Littimer) and her escape from the villa show the spirit she still possesses. And it is Martha, dedicated to helping Mr. Peggotty in his search, who finally finds Emily and brings her uncle to her. Both, under Mr. Peggotty's protection, are redeemed in Australia. Dickens has certainly put the fates of the "fallen" girl and the prostitute "in a new and pathetic way" and may well have done "some good"; but it is disappointing that, in a novel of so much freshness and spontaneity of language, he should have had recourse in their most emotional moments to the set scenes and stilted speeches of melodrama.

David Copperfield has relatively little of the hollow "society" epitomized in *Dombey and Son* by the Hon. Mrs. Skewton and Major Joey Bagstock in Leamington and, in *Bleak House,* by the aristocratic hangers-on at Chesney Wold. But Dickens could not resist giving David the experience of one fashionable dinner party, given by Wickfield's London agent, Mr. Waterbrook, and his formidable wife (Chapter 25). It is a short scene, but the satire is deadly. "The dinner was very long, and the conversation was about the Aristocracy—and Blood. Mrs. Waterbrook repeatedly told us, that if she had a weakness, it was Blood." Another lady—christened "Hamlet's aunt" by David because of her black velvet dress and hat—takes the adulation further: "There are some low minds . . . that would prefer to do what *I* should call bow down before idols. Positively idols! Before services, intellect, and so on. But these are intangible points. Blood is not so. We see Blood in a nose, and we know it."

The bizarre dialogue that follows, when the ladies have left the table, is aimed to mystify and discomfort the young David and Traddles and is beautifully enacted, a mixture of realism and fantasy; Dickens has perfectly caught its portentous tone: "'Do you mean the D. of A.'s?' said Mr. Spiker. 'The C. of B.'s!' said Mr. Gulpidge. Mr. Spiker raised his eyebrow, and looked much concerned. 'When the question was referred to Lord—I needn't name him,' said Mr. Gulpidge, checking himself—'I understand,' said Mr. Spiker, 'N.' Mr. Gulpidge darkly nodded—'was referred to him, his answer was, "Money, or no release."' 'Lord bless my soul!' cried Mr. Spiker" (25:374–75).

"Society" holds the stage twice more: first in Chapter 36 in David's account of Jack Maldon's languorous breakfast conversation with Dr. Strong, and then at the end of the novel, in the description of the now married, rich, and fashionable Julia Mills (she is underlined twice in Dickens's memorandum note). "'Is there any news to-day?' inquired the Doctor. 'Nothing at all, sir,' replied Mr. Maldon. 'There's an account about the people being hungry and discontented down in the North, but they are always being hungry and discontented somewhere.' . . . 'There's a long statement in the papers, sir, about a murder,' observed Mr. Maldon. But somebody is always being murdered, and I didn't read it'" (36:524–25).

Jack Maldon is, of course, one of the "society" so described by Julia Mills; the last we hear of him is in his "Patent Office, sneering at the hand that gave it him, and speaking to me of the doctor as 'so charmingly antique'" (64:870). And in both cases, "society" is dismissed for its "professed indifference to everything that can advance or can retard mankind." The elegant ladies and gentleman of *Bleak House*'s Chesney Wold "who agreed to put a smooth glaze on the world, and to keep down all its realities," are not so very far away.

The final target for Dickens's satire in the novel is the model prison system, based on Pentonville (Chapter 62). The appearance there of Uriah Heep and Littimer as the two model prisoners and of Creakle as presiding magistrate has been discussed already (Chapter 5). The self-exposure of such blatant hypocrisy was one of Dickens's consummate arts. But the description of the prison itself and, above all, of the "system" on which it is regulated is, with all its scorn and sarcasm, a passionate piece of social criticism. The details he attacked—the system's vast expense, the "supreme comfort of prisoners," the lavish meals, the delusion that the prisoners know nothing of each other—are precisely those he had attacked six months before in his *Household Words* article, "Pet Prisoners" (see Chapter 5). Dickens had strongly disapproved of the so-called separate system in prisons after he visited the Eastern Penitentiary near Philadelphia in March 1842 and was shocked by its mental effects on prisoners; in

England it was a topical, highly controversial issue. To introduce such an issue seems quite alien to the spirit of *David Copperfield*; as we remember the comparatively casual tone of some of its other, scattered satire, it seems remarkable that *Bleak House*, with its all-embracing topicality and very different spirit, was not more than a year away.

Chapter Eleven

The Use of Fairy Tale

It is impossible to write about the profound importance to *David Copperfield* of the use of fairy-tale and storybook enchantment without acknowledging a substantial debt to Harry Stone's central chapter, "David Copperfield: The Fairy-Tale Method Perfected," in his *Dickens and the Invisible World,* and this I happily do. As he rightly insists, Dickens's achievement here is one of fusion: the storybook enchantment blends with the intense realism of the novel and, in the process, both enriches and deepens it. Not only does a sense of enchantment lie over the idyllic early scenes of David with his mother and Peggotty, and a sense of nightmare over the scenes with the Murdstones and the trials of David's flight to Dover, but many of the key characters are given a new depth by this kind of treatment. Betsey Trotwood has the fully realistic power of the indomitable eccentric; but she is also David's fairy godmother. Mr. Dick may be there to show the value of the humane treatment of idiots, but he is also the Holy Fool. The "Good and Bad Angels" of the title of Chapter 25 are clearly Agnes and Steerforth. Uriah Heep, with his red hair, red eyes, and writhings, has a more than realistic malignancy. Certain scenes have a far more than naturalistic power: above all, the storm at Yarmouth—"Tempest" in the chapter heading, with its conscious or unconscious echo of Lear's "tempest in my mind"—and its driving at similarly apocalyptic effects in its striking sense of doom.

The treatment of Betsey Trotwood in the novel's first chapter shows the blend at once: realistically, she is imperious, short-tempered, a terror both to David's mother and to little Mr. Chillip, who is attending her. But one incident quickly establishes her real self: David's mother, at her request, lets her hair fall down and in "a short pause which ensued, she had a fancy that she felt Miss Betsey touch her hair, and that with no ungentle hand." And a few moments later, convinced that the child about to be born will be a girl, Betsey says, "From the moment of this girl's birth, child, I intend to be her friend. I intend to be her godmother." When it's a boy, she "vanished like a discontented fairy . . . and never came back any more" (1:12). But her true status is now assured. Her sudden entry, in the glow of the setting sun, her touch of David's mother's hair, her equally sudden departure "like a discontented fairy"—all point to a magical quality in her, obscured as it is by her eccentric abruptness. "Discontented" she may be now, but it is her touch of his mother's hair that keeps David going on the nightmare Dover Road. And it is as David's fairy godmother that we shall see her.

Formidable as she remains on the surface, that will indeed be her role throughout the novel: exorciser of the malignant Murdstones; supplier of all David's needs—including giving him his new name; tester of his character, when she loses her money; tester and prober, again, when he chooses Dora instead of Agnes for his wife; hysterically (for the only time, says David) happy when he finally marries Agnes. As a totally trusting relationship, it is central to the novel and movingly done. But the strong suggestion that there is a magical quality to it—that Betsey *cannot* let her godchild down—adds to its weight. In a novel with its quota of unsatisfactory parents—the Murdstones and Mrs. Steerforth, above all, but David's poor mother is hardly adequate in her trials—Betsey Trotwood shines out as both surrogate mother and fairy godmother. She is something of a fairy godmother to Mr. Dick, too: she has released him from the fate of imprisonment in an asylum, treats him as not only sane but wise, and fully earns his trust in her as "the most extraordinary woman in the world." The climax of his instinctive understanding—his reconciliation of Dr. Strong and Annie—has something of the wisdom of the Holy Fool in it. As joint guardian with Betsey of David, he shares—simple as he is in worldly terms—something of the magical quality of her devotion.

There is certainly a strong fairy-tale element in David's innocent boyhood love for little Emily. From the beginning he idolizes her; his fancy, he says, "etherealised, and made a very angel of her." The gifts she would give to Mr. Peggotty, were she to become "a lady," come straight out of a fairy story: "a sky-blue coat with diamond buttons, nankeen trousers, a red velvet waistcoat, a cocked hat, a large gold watch, a silver pipe, and a box of money" (3:35). David himself is enchanted when he returns and reads to her in the doorway of the boat; he has "never beheld such sky, such water, such glorified ships sailing away into golden air." And the fairy-tale enchantment continues when he fantasizes over their marrying, "never growing older, never growing wiser, children ever." But the fantasy ends with a different kind of fairy story, an allusion to *The Babes in the Wood:* "laying down our heads on moss at night . . . and buried by the birds when we were dead!" (10:147). The pentameter there underlines Dickens's own emotion. Harry Stone is surely right in seeing the allusion going both ways: back to his own childhood fantasy of being abandoned by his parents; forward in its ironical prediction of changes and deaths to come (234). But the allusion is not developed, and David is soon the fairy-tale hero again, the sole protector of Emily and Mrs. Gummidge, only wishing "that a lion or a serpent, or any ill-disposed monster, would make an attack upon us," that he could destroy him "and cover myself with glory" (10:148). Like a storybook hero, David dreams of dragons all night.

But the blend of realism and the supernatural (here, the infernal) is at its strongest in the novel's three most malign characters: the Murdstones and Uriah Heep.

There is no question of the realism of either Mr. Murdstone or his sister. He is the gloomy, tyrannical, cruel husband and stepfather, portrayed in several Victorian memoirs as well as in fiction; she, the interfering, aggressive, sexually frustrated spinster, who might have become a caricature. But neither is a caricature, because of the sheer power of their malignity, which, in its relentlessness and concentration (they seem to have no other life), is sufficiently unnatural as to be diabolical. Each is given key images to suggest this. Mr. Murdstone is analogous to the dog—"deep-mouthed and black-haired like Him" he seems to the young David (the capital letter suggests both his revulsion from his new "father" and the satanic ancestry he gives him); five chapters—and considerable suffering—later, the dog has become an image, ironically used by David for them both: "He ordered me like a dog, and I obeyed like a dog" (8:119). Miss Murdstone not only resembles her brother, she abets him on every occasion, above all, in attacking any demonstration of love shown by David's mother or by David himself. Her metallic imagery, blackly comic, is frightening enough. But her horror when David picks his stepbrother up and when David's mother sees a likeness between her two children goes further: it is a total denial of love between parents and children.

Murdstone's sadism, again, goes beyond the human. It begins at once, in almost the first words he addresses to David: "'David,' he said, making his lips thin, by pressing them together, 'if I have an obstinate horse or dog to deal with, what do you think I do?' 'I don't know.' 'I beat him. . . . I make him wince, and smart. I say to myself, "I'll conquer that fellow"; and if it were to cost him all the blood he had, I should do it'" (4:46).

His beating of David—after the biting, "as if he would have beaten me to death"—comes as hardly a surprise.

Before that, as David's lessons become worse and worse, Dickens employs another key image for the Murdstones, operating as a pair: "The influence of the Murdstones upon me was like the fascination of two snakes on a wretched young bird" (4:55). The running title for the text at this point is "I am under a spell." It is clearly an evil spell, and it suggests powerfully a diabolical malignity in the Murdstones that not only deepens their realism but goes beyond it.

Uriah Heep is the most compelling mixture in the novel of realism and the infernal. Physically, with his cadaverous face, red hair, red eyes, "long, lank, skeleton hand," and writhings, he is grotesque; but he is soon established as diabolical, too. One of his first actions we are shown is breathing into the nostrils of the pony that has brought Betsey Trotwood and David, "and immediately covering them with his hand, as if he were putting some spell upon him" (15:219). He has the power, already exhibited at the end of this chapter, of forcing his way into David's fancies and dreams (here as a gargoyle; later, as the victim of David's red-hot poker). Like Milton's Satan, he changes his shape and size at will: "He seemed to swell and grow before my eyes; the room seemed full of the echoes of his voice. And in a sinister version of déja vu, he seems to have the power of even transcending time: "The strange feeling . . . that all this had occurred before, at some indefinite time, and that I knew what he was going to say next, took possession of me" (25:381). He had already reminded David, as he watched Agnes, of "an ugly and rebellious genie watching a good spirit," and when he stays the night at David's London lodgings, the recollection that he was there "oppressed me with a leaden dread, as if I had had some meaner quality of devil for a lodger" (25:383).

There is no question about his infernal origins; the signs and portents of the storybook devil are everywhere. But at the same time, as consummate hypocrite and schemer, he is a realistic study. His hypocrisy and "umbleness" have already been discussed (Chapter 6); his increasing power over Mr. Wickfield is horrible, but entirely convincing. The finale, when he reveals quite explicitly his ambition to marry Agnes, leads to Wickfield's perhaps over-melodramatic outburst; but it also leads to one of the most sinister phrases used of Uriah, bringing together unerringly the realistic and diabolical: "*He* knows best," says Wickfield, "for he has always been at my elbow, whispering me" (39:579). The vision is of Milton's Satan, a toad whispering in Eve's ear; but the phrase also conjures up, momentarily, the full horror of Uriah's campaign. Uriah's very ordinariness when David first meets him (his physical appearance apart)—working in Mr. Wickfield's office by day, studying Tidd's legal textbook at night—compounds that horror. It may remind us of another portrait of the Devil, Ivan's visitor in Dostoyevski's *The Brothers Karamazov*, who comes in the guise of a very ordinary fellow citizen. And we know of Dostoyevski's often-acknowledged debt to Dickens.

Uriah's mother, though a less ubiquitous character than her son, is given a tincture of the diabolical, too, and especially in the scene where they have, like two invading demons, virtually taken over Wickfield's home. Her eye, thinks David, is "an evil eye to the rest of the world" (Uriah apart); it drops "furtively" upon her knitting (which looks like a net), and as she works away, "she showed in the firelight like an ill-looking enchantress, baulked as yet by the radiant goodness opposite [Agnes], but getting ready for a cast of her net by-and-by" (39:571).

The great scene of Uriah's exposure by Micawber has already been discussed (Chapter 6). It is the climax of the plot of Uriah as hypocrite and cheat, and the details of fraud and forgery are lovingly and realistically exhibited; as a theatrical performance by Micawber, it has great comic power. But it is also the banishment of a storybook devil, a mythical act of justice conjured up—if comically—by Micawber's marvelous set of vows, three chapters before, to destroy him, the "serpent," "abandoned rascal," and "transcendent and immortal hypocrite and perjurer."

Steerforth possesses a very different kind of magic, but looking back over the years, David sees it as magic nevertheless. He still believes Steerforth's manner to have borne "a kind of enchantment" with it. He still believes Steerforth, by virtue of his handsomeness, his gifts, and "some inborn power of attraction besides . . . to have carried a spell with him to which it was a natural weakness to yield, and which not many persons could withstand" (7:104). David himself, his *protégé* at Salem House, has no hope of withstanding it: Steerforth answers all the emotional needs of a lonely and soon to be orphaned child. Steerforth's mother, we know, worships him, and Rosa Dartle has adored him. He descends almost like a god of protean power into Mr. Peggotty's family circle on the boat; even Mrs. Gummidge admits she must have been "bewitched" by him. (A passage canceled in proof, for want of space, went further and had her continually laughing as

Steerforth sits beside her and claims to be "a long lorn creetur" himself.)[29] Only Agnes (but she is, of course, a vital exception) mistrusts him and warns David against him as a "bad Angel."

The showing of feet of clay beneath Steerforth's godlike charm is, of course, a major theme of the novel. In purely human terms, we have seen it already at Salem House. But at Yarmouth, where the final exposure of the real Steerforth will take place, Dickens uses a succession of incidents and allusions in a highly Shakespearean way (including Steerforth's momentary identification of himself with Macbeth, already discussed) to prophesy the future. And the suggestion of fate, of a magic very different from Steerforth's charm, now ironically running against him—or at least against the godlike reputation he has built up—is very strong. Two incidents stand out. In the first, David comes upon Steerforth sitting alone before the fire in Mr. Peggotty's boat. His response, when David puts his hand on his shoulder, is excessive: "'You come upon me,' he said, almost angrily, 'like a reproachful ghost!'" David replies, "'Have I called you down from the stars?' 'No,' he answered, 'No.' 'Up from anywhere, then?' . . . 'I was looking at the pictures in the fire,' he returned" (one of Dickens's favorite images for suggesting some kind of preknowledge of the future) (22:321). After striking out "a train of red-hot sparks that went careering up the little chimney," Steerforth bursts out that he has been "thinking that all the people we found so glad on the night of our coming down, might—to judge of from the present wasted air of the place—be dispersed, or dead, or come to I don't know what harm. David, I wish to God I had had a judicious father these last twenty years! . . . I wish with all my soul I had been better guided! . . . I wish with all my soul I could guide myself better!" (22:321–22). And a few moments later, he is even more explicit about his future guilt, about being a storybook villain: "I have been a nightmare to myself, just now. . . . At odd times, nursery tales come up into the memory, unrecognised for what they are" (322).

After the Macbeth allusions and the ominous news that he has bought a boat, the *Stormy Petrel,* and rechristened her the *Little Em'ly,* we have the second incident—the prostitute Martha (as we soon know it is) following Ham and Emily along the beach.

Both these incidents, together with the Macbeth allusions and the rechristening of the boat, add up to a kind of omniscient irony at which Dickens became more and more adept. It is at its most powerful perhaps in *Bleak House,* in Chapter 48, which ends with Tulking-horne's murder. There, the omens—the Dedlocks' splendid clock, his own watch, the figure of the Roman pointing from the ceiling—fail, malevolently we feel, to warn him. Here, Steerforth is on his way to carry out a seduction; he is not the victim of a murder, but Dickens skillfully suggested the presence of fate—and a stronger magic than the magic of Steerforth's charm.

There can be no doubt of the supernatural qualities David ascribes to Agnes, nor of the part that she plays throughout the novel as his "good angel." The trouble is that everything about her is too explicitly good. From David's first association of her with a stained-glass window's "tranquil brightness" to his prayer to her that ends the novel—the prayer to "still find thee near me, pointing upward!"—she is what Coventry Patmore, in his highly influential long poem, labeled "The Angel in the House": the "Womanly Ideal." The role she plays for David as his "sister" is the essentially spiritual one that Mary Hogarth had played for Dickens. Agnes is always there when David needs her: a loving and wise companion to Dora; in her letter to him in Switzerland, a giver of consolation and advice that help to restore him from breakdown; and finally, an image of patience that will wait to the novel's end to tell him that she has loved him all her life. Like Mary Hogarth, she has "no faults." But in a novel that contains Dora's extremely human sexual warmth and provocativeness, such supernatural goodness can only disappoint.

Chapter Twelve
A Note on the Pathetic Fallacy

Of the great Victorian novelists, Dickens used what John Ruskin called "the pathetic fallacy" (the ascription of human feelings to nature) the most. "What the Waves were always saying" is an integral theme of *Dombey and Son,* and from the fog in *Bleak House* to the river Thames in *Our Mutual Friend,* nature increasingly reflects the plight of numerous characters. Both the sea and the river play their "pathetic" parts in *Copperfield;* in "Absence" (Chapter 58), the account of David's sojourn in Switzerland, Dickens made the part played by nature paramount again.

An early example of the pathetic fallacy is the treatment of the elms at Blunderstone, in Chapter 1, just before David is born: they bend to each other "like giants who were whispering secrets" and fall "into a violent flurry, tossing their wild arms about, as if their late confidences were really too wicked for their peace of mind." But any sinister omen intended by this is not explicitly developed at this point.

The sea, however, in its many guises, is central to the novel: comic at the very beginning, because David is born with a caul, a guarantee against drowning (more grim than comic, when we remember the fates of Steerforth and Ham); cruel and fearful to little Emily, as she and David, as children, pick up stones on the Yarmouth beach; brightly hopeful to young David, as he lies in bed on his first night at his aunt's, hoping to read his fortune in the moonlight on the water; hungry for them in its roaring, as Steerforth says to David (with obvious irony), as they walk towards Mr. Peggotty's boat. Yet more obviously an omen is the sealike mist that rises in the valley below Highgate (as David leaves Mrs. Steerforth and Rosa Dartle in Chapter 46) and makes it seem "as if the gathering waters would encompass them." This is the end of a number, and Dickens, with his skill in creating suspense, makes David add, "I have reason to remember this, and think of it with awe; for before I looked upon those two again, a stormy sea had risen to their feet" (46:673–74).

The stormy sea that destroys Steerforth and Ham in Chapter 55 is treated apocalyptically as well as realistically. The terror it causes David is more than rational: it is "a new and indefinable horror," and when he shakes off the lethargy that binds him to his chair in the inn, his whole frame "thrilled with objectless and unintelligible fear" (790). The bell ringing on the doomed ship both anticipates Steerforth's death and suggests rightful retribution. Ham's last words to David, "Mas'r Davy . . . if my time is come, 'tis come. If 'tan't, I'll bide it" (793), point to the opposite: to the stoicism of the essentially noble sufferer.

The river comes in only one scene, Martha's intended suicide (Chapter 47). Dickens certainly uses the pathetic fallacy here ("'I know it's like me,' she exclaims. 'I know that I belong to it.'" [681]); but any extra poignancy that the device can bring—and, at its best, does bring—is lost in the conventional "fallen woman" rhetoric that Dickens deployed here.

It is difficult not to see the direct influence of Wordsworth (see Chapter 1), with his strong belief in the pathetic fallacy, in Chapter 58, the account of nature's healing power over David in his grief and desolation, as he seeks solace in the Swiss mountains. But David's assertions sound too explicit, even portentous: "All at once, in this serenity, great Nature spoke to me; and soothed me to lay down my weary head upon the grass, and weep as I had not wept yet, since Dora died!" (815); and "I resorted humbly whither Agnes had commended me; I sought out Nature, never sought in vain" (816). Dickens's way was not Wordsworth's way, nor does his prose here evoke Wordsworth's visionary "spots of time"; and we miss both the sharpness and immediacy of the novel's early scenes and the irony that plays round much of the rest. Successful completion of David's pilgrimage—the hope of all bildungsromanen—was clearly of the greatest importance to Dickens; but it is the trials and errors on the way, and the intensity with which they are experienced and re-created, that have made *David Copperfield* so greatly loved a novel.

Notes and References

1. Lord Shaftesbury to John Forster, Forster Collection, Victoria and Albert Museum, London.

2. *Early Victorian England*, 2 vols., ed. G. M. Young (London: Oxford University Press, 1934), 2:460.

3. *The Letters of Charles Dickens*, 3 vols., ed. Walter Dexter (London: Nonesuch Press, 1938), 3:438; hereafter cited in the text as *Letters* (Nonesuch).

4. Peter Coveney, *The Images of Childhood* (Harmondsworth, Eng.: Penguin, 1967), formerly entitled *Poor Monkey: The Child in Literature* (London: Rockcliff, 1957).

5. *The Letters of Charles Dickens*, vol. 1 (Pilgrim ed.), ed. Madeline House and Graham Storey (Oxford: Clarendon, 1965), 639: hereafter cited in the text as *Letters* 1.

6. Dennis Walder, *Dickens and Religion* (London: Allen & Unwin, 1981), 2.

7. Given in Philip Collins, *Dickens and Education* (London: Macmillan, 1963), 114–15.

8. John Forster, *The Life of Charles Dickens*, ed. J. W. T. Ley (London: Cecil Palmer, 1928), 525–24; hereafter cited in the text as Forster.

9. *The Letters of Charles Dickens*, vol. 6 (Pilgrim ed.), ed. Graham Storey, Kathleen Tillotson, and Nina Burgis (Oxford: Clarendon, 1988), 195; hereafter cited in the text as *Letters* 6.

10. Sylvère Monod, *Dickens Romancier* (Paris: Hachette, 1953), translated by the author as *Dickens the Novelist* (Norman: University of Oklahoma Press, 1968).

11. *Letters and Private Papers of W. M. Thackeray*, ed. Gordon N. Ray (London: Oxford University Press, 1945), 2:531–533; *The Brontës: Their Lives, Friendships, and Correspondence*, ed. T. J. Wise and J. A. Symington (Oxford: Basil Blackwell, 1932), 3:20; *Harriet Martineau's Autobiography* (London: Smith, Elder, 1877), 2:378–79.

12. Matthew Arnold, "The Incompatibles," *Nineteenth Century* (June 1881).

13. Edmund Wilson, "Dickens: The Two Scrooges," in *The Wound and the Bow* (London: Secker & Warburg, 1941).

14. "David Copperfield," in *Dickens and the Twentieth Century,* ed. John Gross and Gabriel Pearson (London: Routledge & Kegan Paul, 1962).

15. Michael Slater, *Dickens and Women* (London: Dent, 1983), 63–64, 100.

16. Thackeray, *Letters and Private Papers,* 2:772.

17. Harry Stone, *Dickens and the Invisible World* (Bloomington: Indiana University Press, 1979; London: Macmillan, 1980), ch. 7; Allan Grant, *A Preface to Dickens* (London: Longmans, 1984), 109.

18. Michael Allen, *Charles Dickens' Childhood* (London: Macmillan, 1988).

19. *The Letters of Charles Dickens,* vol. 5 (Pilgrim ed.), ed. Graham Storey and K. J. Fielding (Oxford: Clarendon, 1981), 559; hereafter cited in the text as *Letters 5.*

20. John Butt and Kathleen Tillotson, *Dickens at Work* (London: Methuen, 1957), 130.

21. See particularly Gwendolyn B. Needham, "The Undisciplined Heart of David Copperfield," *Nineteenth-Century Fiction* 9 (1954).

22. Thomas Carlyle, *Latter-Day Pamphlets* (March 1850).

23. Given in *The Letters of Charles Dickens,* vol. 3 (Pilgrim ed.), ed. Madeline House, Graham Storey, and Kathleen Tillotson (Oxford: Clarendon, 1974), 336n; hereafter cited in the text as *Letters 3.*

24. See Nina Burgis, Introduction to *David Copperfield,* ed. Nina Burgis (Oxford: Clarendon, 1981), xxxiv.

25. V. S. Pritchett, *The Living Novel* (London: Chatto & Windus, 1946), 78.

26. As Margaret Cardwell has convincingly shown in the *Dickensian* 56 (1960):29–33.

27. George Ford, Introduction to the Riverside edition of *David Copperfield* (Boston: Houghton Mifflin, 1958), reprinted in *The Dickens Critics,* ed. George H. Ford and Lauriat Lane, Jr. (Ithaca, N.Y.: Cornell University Press, 1961).

28. Angus Wilson, "Dickens: A Haunting," *Critical Quarterly* (Summer 1960), reprinted in Ford and Lane, *The Dickens Critics.*

29. The whole passage is given in Nina Burgis, *David Copperfield,* 270n.

Bibliography

Primary Sources

New Oxford Illustrated Dickens, 21 vols., London: Oxford University Press, 1948–58.

David Copperfield (New Oxford Illustrated Dickens), Oxford: Oxford University Press, 1948; latest reprint, 1987.

David Copperfield (Riverside edition), ed. G. H. Ford, Boston: Houghton Mifflin, 1958.

David Copperfield (Clarendon Dickens), ed. Nina Burgis, Oxford: Clarendon, 1981.

Household Words, "conducted" by Charles Dickens, 30 March 1850–28 May 1859, 19 vols.

The Letters of Charles Dickens (Nonesuch edition), 3 vols., ed. Walter Dexter, London: Nonesuch Press, 1938.

The Letters of Charles Dickens (Pilgrim edition), vols. 1–6 (1820–52), gen. eds., Madeline House, Graham Storey, and Kathleen Tillotson, Oxford: Clarendon, 1965–88.

Dickens: The Public Readings, ed. Philip Collins, Oxford: Clarendon, 1975.

Secondary Sources

Books

Michael Allen, *Charles Dickens' Childhood,* London: Macmillan, 1988. Gives important new evidence on Dickens's childhood homes and on the length of his employment in Warren's blacking-warehouse—considerably longer than had hitherto been generally thought.

J. H. Buckley, in *Season of Youth: The Bildungsroman from Dickens to Golding*, Cambridge, Mass.: Harvard University Press, 1974. Chapter 2, "Dickens, David, and Pip," is the best account of *David Copperfield* as bildungsroman.

John Butt and Kathleen Tillotson, *Dickens at Work*, London: Methuen, 1957; reprinted 1963 and 1968. Includes "David Copperfield Month by Month," drawn on extensively in this study.

John Carey, *The Violent Effigy: A Study of Dickens' Imagination*, London: Faber, 1973. Contains the stimulating and provocative chapters, "Dickens's Children" and "Dickens and Sex."

A. O. J. Cockshut, *The Imagination of Dickens*, London: Collins, 1961. Discusses *David Copperfield* as a blend of nostalgic realism and fantasy.

Philip Collins, *Dickens and Education*, London: Macmillan, 1963. Very useful on the background to the two schools in *David Copperfield*.

———, ed., *Dickens: The Critical Heritage*, London: Routledge & Kegan Paul, 1971. Includes a wide selection of the contemporary reviews of *David Copperfield*.

Peter Coveney, *Poor Monkey: The Child in Literature*, London: Rockcliff, 1957; new ed. entitled *The Images of Childhood*, Harmondsworth: Penguin, 1967. Shows, particularly in two chapters, "From Coleridge to Dickens" and "The Child in Dickens," that Dickens's treatment of children is central.

K. J. Fielding, *Charles Dickens*, London: Longmans, 1958; 2d ed., 1965. An excellent critical introduction to the novels.

George H. Ford, *Dickens and His Readers*, Princeton, N. J.: Princeton University Press, 1955. The most useful study for the general critical reception of the novels.

——— and Lauriat Lane, Jr., eds., *The Dickens Critics*, Ithaca, N.Y.: Cornell University Press, 1961. Contains the best-known essays on Dickens, of which G. H. Ford, "David Copperfield" [Introduction to the Riverside edition, 1958], Humphry House, "The Macabre Dickens," George Orwell, "Charles Dickens," V. S. Pritchett, "The Comic World of Dickens," George Santayana, "Dickens," Dorothy Van Ghent, "The Dickens World," and Lionel Trilling, "Little Dorrit," are all most helpful.

John Forster, *The Life of Charles Dickens*, 3 vols., 1872–74, ed. J. W. T. Ley, 1 vol., London: Cecil Palmer, 1928. The standard biography by his closest friend.

Robert Garis, *The Dickens Theatre*, Oxford: Clarendon, 1965. The best study of Dickens's theatrical style.

Allan Grant, *A Preface to Dickens*, London: Longmans, 1984. An excellent introduction in the Longmans Preface Books.

Bibliography

Graham Greene, *Lost Childhood and Other Essays*, London: Eyre & Spotis-woode, 1951. Part 2, Chapter 6, "The Young Dickens," is a very perceptive study.

Humphry House, *The Dickens World*, London: Oxford University Press, 1941; reprinted 1960. Indispensable for the historical background.

Edgar Johnson, *Charles Dickens: His Tragedy and Triumph*, 2 vols., New York: Simon & Schuster, 1952; rev. ed., without the critical chapters, 1 vol., London: Allen Lane, 1977. Incorporates much more material than Forster was able to use.

John Jones, "David Copperfield," in *Dickens and the Twentieth Century*, ed. John Gross and Gabriel Pearson, London: Routledge & Kegan Paul, 1976. Particularly good on the young David Copperfield.

Fred Kaplan, *Dickens: A Biography*, London: Hodder & Stoughton, 1988. The latest life.

Robert Langton, *The Childhood and Youth of Charles Dickens*, enlarged and rev. ed., London: Hutchinson, 1891. Still very useful on the young Dickens.

F. R. and Q. D. Leavis, *Dickens the Novelist*, London: Chatto & Windus, 1970. Contains a challenging essay by Q. D. Leavis on *David Copperfield*.

Norman and Jeanne Mackenzie, *Dickens: A Life*, London: Oxford University Press, 1979. Like Edgar Johnson's biography, incorporates much more material than Forster could use.

J. Hillis Miller, *Charles Dickens: The World of His Novels*, Cambridge, Mass.: Harvard University Press, 1958. Discusses *David Copperfield* in terms of Dickens's treatment of romantic love.

Sylvère Monod, *Dickens Romancier*, Paris: Hachette, 1953; translated by the author, *Dickens the Novelist*, Norman: University of Oklahoma Press, 1968. Part 3, "At the Top," devotes five chapters to *David Copperfield*, including "Autobiographical Reality and Invention" and "Dickens's Language and Style."

Michael Slater, *Dickens and Women*, London: Dent, 1983. Examines the women both in Dickens's life and in his novels; very helpful on *David Copperfield*.

Harry Stone, *Dickens and the Invisible World*, Bloomington, Ind.: 1979, London: Macmillan, 1980. A study of the effect of fairy tales and myths on Dickens's art; drawn on extensively in Chapter 10 of this study.

H. P. Sucksmith, *The Narrative Art of Charles Dickens*, Oxford: Clarendon, 1970. Uses the manuscripts, number plans, and corrected proofs of the novels to show Dickens as a highly conscious artist.

Kathleen Tillotson, *Novels of the Eighteen Forties*, Oxford: Clarendon, 1954; reissued with corrections, London: Oxford University Press, 1961.

Includes a chapter on *Dombey and Son* that is very helpful to a study of *David Copperfield*.

Dennis Walder, *Dickens and Religion*, London: Allen & Unwin, 1981. Shows the importance to his creative imagination of his religious beliefs.

Alexander Welsh, *The City of Dickens*, Oxford: Clarendon, 1971. Treats the city as both historical reality and metaphor.

Angus Wilson, *The World of Charles Dickens*, London: Secker & Warburg, 1970. Particularly good on children and childhood in Dickens.

Edmund Wilson, *The Wound and the Bow*, Boston: Houghton Mifflin, 1941. "Dickens: The Two Scrooges" is still one of the most influential essays on Dickens.

Articles

C. B. Cox, "Realism and Fantasy in *David Copperfield*," *Bulletin of the John Rylands Library* 12 (1970).

Angus Easson, "John Dickens and the Navy Pay Office," *Dickensian* 70 (1974).

Albert D. Hutter, "Reconstructive Autobiography: The Experience of Warren's blacking," *Dickens Studies Annual* 11 (1977).

Christopher Mulvey, "David Copperfield: The Folk-Story Structure," *Dickens Studies Annual* 5 (1976).

Gwendolyn B. Needham, "The Undisciplined Heart of David Copperfield," *Nineteenth-Century Fiction* 9 (1954).

Harry Stone, "Fairy Tales and Ogres: Dickens's Imagination and *David Copperfield*," *Criticism* 6 (1964).

Kathleen Tillotson, "The Middle Years: From the *Carol* to *Copperfield*," *Dickens Memorial Lectures: The Dickens Fellowship* (1970).

Bibliographies, etc.

Nicolas Bentley, Michael Slater, and Nina Burgis, *The Dickens Index*, London: Oxford University Press, 1988.

Philip Collins, "Charles Dickens," in *The New Cambridge Bibliography of English Literature*, Cambridge: Cambridge University Press, 1969.

"Charles Dickens" in *Victorian Fiction: A Second Guide to Research*, ed. George H. Ford, New York: Modern Language Association, 1978.

Ada Nisbet, "Charles Dickens," in *Victorian Fiction: A Guide to Research*, ed. Lionel Stevenson, Cambridge, Mass.: Harvard University Press, 1964.

Norman Page, *A Dickens Chronology*, London: Macmillan, 1988.

Index

The Author

Graham Storey has recently retired as reader in English, University of Cambridge, and staff fellow of Trinity Hall, of which he is now an emeritus fellow. He has been general editor with the late Madeline House and Kathleen Tillotson of the Pilgrim edition of Dickens's letters since 1965 and has coedited volumes 1, 2, 3, 5, and 6. He is author of a study of *Bleak House* in the Landmarks of World Literature series (Cambridge: Cambridge University Press, 1987); contributed "Dickens: The Regress of the Radical" to *Dickens and Other Victorians* (Essays in Honour of Philip Collins), ed. Joanne Shattock (London: Macmillan, 1988); and recently contributed "A Tale of Two Cities" (on *A Tale* and *Barnaby Rudge*) to the London Exhibition to mark the bicentenary of the French Revolution. He also completed the editing of G. M. Hopkins's *Journals and Papers* (Oxford: Oxford University Press, 1959) on the death of Humphry House; has edited *Hopkins: A Selection*, New Oxford English Series (Oxford: Oxford University Press, 1967); and is the author of *A Preface to Hopkins* London: Longmans, 1981). He has lectured on Dickens in Europe, America, and Japan.